It's All Possible

How to lead an *epic life* and unleash the *high performance hero* within you

Rob Hartnett

Praise for *It's All Possible*

Rob Hartnett is passionate about all he does and is a master communicator when it comes to spreading his enthusiasm. He never fails to inspire everyone, as he is bound to do with this book.

As the basis of his success Rob is the complete, devoted family man... he understands and truly appreciates the important things that guide his life.

Alistair Murray AM – Chairman Ronstan International

Rob has interwoven stories and insights from some of the most famous people in the world – along with his own personal experiences across business, sport, parenting and friendship – sharing his learnings, systems and wisdom for our benefit, showing us how we, too, can lead a fulfilling life. Rob tells us that leading a great life is about having a purpose and it takes effort and determination and nothing happens by chance. But the most important lesson is that at the heart of everything in life is love and relationships.

Sue Barrett – Selling better strategist, educator and advocate, CEO of Barrett.com.au, and author of *142 Days of Gratitude That Changed My Life Forever*

Rob Hartnett has developed a translatable model for anyone wanting to achieve their goals and better manage change through his remarkable intellect, diligence and persistence. Rob helps endorse creating better environments that support mental health and well-being, recognising that loving ourselves translates directly into doing what we love.

Rae Bonney – Integrated wellbeing specialist/speaker/radio presenter/men's issues advocate/suicide prevention counsellor

Rob's book offers rich insights from experts and his personal experience to show us all how we can climb our own mountains, grow, and use our grey matter more effectively. If you are looking for wisdom combined with practical insights, this is the book for you. Legsellent stuff.

Hannah MacDougall PhD, B Sp and ExSc, B Com. with Honours – Elite cyclist, motivational speaker, expert in athlete well-being

A must-read on how to improve your performance and lead an epic life. *It's All Possible* is an insightful, motivational and captivating book that is easy to read and will inspire you to greatness.

Thomas J. Williams – Chairman and founder, Strategic Dynamics Inc, co-author of the Sellers Challenge and Buyer Centred Selling

Rob has been a tremendous partner on our change journey. Change can be hard. The spoils go to those who embrace it. This book will be an invaluable companion to myself and the wonderful team of Possibility Seekers at Vanguard.

Matthew Lumsden – Head of Distribution, Vanguard Investments Australia Ltd

What a motivating, positive read! I was instantly hooked on the real-life examples from Rob on the importance of having an open mind and continually and deliberately investing in my own development. I really like Rob's whole of life approach, covering family, career, hobbies, passion, health and well-being.

David Sturt – Head Coach, TheHurtBox cycling coaching

The greatest don't look at the impossible as a dream but as a destination… *It's All Possible!* Open yourself to create your path, no-one ever achieves anything without having a crack.

Lance Picioane – CEO, Love Me Love You Organisation and former champion AFL player

From someone who has chased their dreams and made them a reality, it's awesome to see such a helpful and inspiring book showing the intricacies of goal-setting and following through.

Tom Burton – Olympic Gold Medallist in sailing, World and multi-Australian champion yachtsman

Whether you are from Melbourne Australia or Melbourne Florida, *It's All Possible* shows that with desire, discipline and determination you can achieve all that you wish for.

Paul Martinelli – International speaker and coach

It's All Possible … What a great mantra for life and in this exceptionally well-written book Rob shares his insights and ideas to propel you towards achieving what's important, what matters and what makes all the difference.

Keith Abraham – Best-selling author and multi-award-winning keynote speaker

It's All Possible is an amazing everyday-applicable compass to navigate your life into all that can be possible for you! With this book, my friend Rob will help you to fulfil your desires, dreams and visions that look impossible. He himself, with all his circumstances has paved the way for you, you just have to take action and follow it!

Nathanael Zurbrügg – Global inspirational speaker, CEO and founder of Unlimit You and Live Life to the Fullest

A powerful resource for anyone wanting to elevate their potential. Rob not only gives you the facts, but the practical strategies that will make all the difference to your high performance life!

Steph Lowe – The Natural Nutritionist, author of *The Real Food Athlete* and *Low Carb Healthy Fat Nutrition*

It's All Possible is a highly readable and fantastically relatable book that gives you everything you need to land your impossible dream, in a simple and practical way. Seriously well done!

Alisa Camplin – Olympic aerial skiing Gold and Bronze Medallist, global resilience and high performance consultant

Rob's 4-Step Possibility System© is brilliant and easy to follow. The use of personal anecdotes throughout the book makes it a very engaging read, while the tools and processes can be readily applied to business as well as personal situations and opportunities.

Sam Mutimer – CEO, Thinktank Social

I have read a great number of books over the years for my continual personal and professional development and I can say that without a doubt *It's All Possible* is one of my top favourites. Rob recognises that for most people the problem is their mindset and when that changes their whole life changes in the space of a month, week, a day, even a second and that is what this book helps you do.

Fiori Giovanni – author of *Defy Your Destiny*, speaker and coach

'My life is a testament to believing that if you want something, you can make it happen. I think what you just have to tell people is, it's all possible.'

Stevie Nicks

'When you grow up in the suburbs of Sydney or Auckland, or Newcastle like Ridley [Scott] or Jamie Bell, a dream like this seems vaguely ludicrous and completely unattainable. But for anybody who's on the down side of advantage and relying purely on courage, it's possible.'

Russell Crowe

'People rise out of the ashes because, at some point, they are invested with a belief in the possibility of triumph over seemingly impossible odds.'

Robert Downey Jr

First published in 2019 by Major Street Publishing Pty Ltd
PO Box 106, Highett, Vic. 3190
E: info@majorstreet.com.au
W: majorstreet.com.au
M: +61 421 707 983

Quantity sales. Special discounts are available on quantity purchases by corporations, associations and others. For details, contact Lesley Williams using the contact details above.

Individual sales. Major Street publications are available through most bookstores. They can also be ordered directly from Major Street's online bookstore at www.majorstreet.com.au.

Orders for university textbook/course adoption use. For orders of this nature, please contact Lesley Williams using the contact details above.

The moral rights of the author have been asserted.

A catalogue record for this book is available from the National Library of Australia

NATIONAL LIBRARY OF AUSTRALIA

ISBN: 978-0-6485159-1-3

Cover design by Simone Geary
Internal design by Production Works
Printed in Australia by Ovato, an Accredited ISO AS/NZS 14001:2004 Environmental Management System Printer.

10 9 8 7 6 5 4 3 2 1

Disclaimer: The material in this publication is in the nature of general comment only, and neither purports nor intends to be advice. Readers should not act on the basis of any matter in this publication without considering (and if appropriate taking) professional advice with due regard to their own particular circumstances. The author and publisher expressly disclaim all and any liability to any person, whether a purchaser of this publication or not, in respect of anything and the consequences of anything done or omitted to be done by any such person in reliance, whether whole or partial, upon the whole or any part of the contents of this publication.

Contents

Acknowledgements

It's All Possible was not hard to write. That's because I didn't *have* to write it, I was *given* the *opportunity* to write it. When I finished it, I was already missing it. I have many more stories to tell, and even more coming that I don't even know about yet. But a book must come to an end, or it won't be published – and that's not a great outcome for anyone. So, here we are.

A book, like life, may seem like it would all be down to the author but it rarely, if ever, is. Let me begin first and foremost by acknowledging my wife, business and life partner, Leisa. Leisa has encouraged me, supported me and assisted greatly with the proofreading and edits of this book.

My middle son, Finn: how blessed am I to have a film screen-writer and dual dux of media to help me. Finn assisted greatly with the editing process; he critiqued an early draft and provided me with a series of suggestions and directions that were invaluable. (I was, at first, impressed by his speed reading, but I was wrong – he was only up to page 10. You should have seen his list by page 80!) Finn has also been vital as a producer and contributor to my podcast, *The Art of the Possible*.

To my other sons, Ben and Lachie, who impress me every day with their achievements and behaviour as young men and keep me well-informed of social media trends, memes and music. Their passion for creativity and design ensure I am always challenged to look at things from a new angle.

Many thanks to my publisher, Lesley Williams, for believing I had something to say – despite the fact that as a writer I make a good speaker. Lesley also had the wisdom to connect me with editor to the stars (and other people like me, who have ideas and stories but who clearly drifted off in English class), the wonderful Brooke Lyons. Thank you, Brooke, for bringing this book to life.

To the wonderful people at the John Maxwell Team (JMT) for being the most positive, proactive, supportive organisation I have worked with. So much of the work from Dr John C Maxwell, Paul Martinelli and Mark Cole keeps me going, and the JMT family provides inspiration continually. To all the people featured in this book, thank you for your time, your inspiration and for doing what you do. Each of us has a unique story to tell, and I was happy to bring some of yours alive so that others may be inspired.

To the wonderful characters at two great cafés where much of the book was written: Simon and Betty at Café ODO, who provide a thriving environment of cyclists, sailors, coffee and conversation; and Giacomo D'Imperio at Da Giacomo Caffe, where our banter on Formula 1 and MotoGP was just the distraction I needed after hitting the keyboard for many hours on end.

Preface

It is 5.50am and I have to snap out of thinking about how to start this book. I am hurtling along at 40km per hour in darkness, just centimetres behind Michelle's rear wheel – it's throwing up sprays of water, which look like sparkling diamonds in my headlight. All I can hear is the whirring of the electric gear shifters as we change gears, and the ominous threat of a car or truck about to pass. I'm pondering chapter outlines when I notice I have missed David's rear wheel passing by. I accelerate by getting off the saddle and punching the pedals, to ensure the training group maintains its rhythm and speed. We all want to complete the 80km ride before work. Most of all I have to catch up before our coach, Steggles, sees that I am lagging. (Although no doubt he will pick it up later, when he notices the spike in my heart rate while conducting his post-session data analysis. I love data and hate data. It can ruin a good story at coffee later when some smart alec checks your results.)

When I am cycling, rolling turns in what appears to be a well-rehearsed sequence with 20 other riders, I truly know I am alive. We have faith in each other and the world, wearing only a small amount of lycra for protection against the wind, the cold and the workers in cars getting an early start. It is an honour to be here.

I bought my first road bike three-and-a-half years prior to this. Back then, a big ride was 10km at about 20km per hour. I'd have to desperately try to remember how to unclip my feet from the pedals when the traffic lights changed. In the years since I have done criterium racing, road racing and time trial, and I have raced overseas and interstate. I have also fallen behind my cycling friends (described as 'getting dropped') more times than I can count, fallen off multiple times, been hit by a car, run out of food and water and learned how to shave my legs. (That last one has given my wonderful wife Leisa and I another topic to battle over: 'Who used the last of the shaving cream?!')

I have seen Tasmanian Richie Porte on one of his five (to date) wins up Willunga Hill in Adelaide – an epic stage of the Tour Down Under. That was an experience right up there with being at the Melbourne Cricket Ground when your Australian Football League team wins the premiership, which I also experienced in 1993. (Go Bombers!)

But don't worry: this is not a cycling book. This is a book about personal leadership, human potential, being your best and achieving all you want out of this precious life we have been blessed with. That said, even in that cycling experience I recount at the beginning of this introduction there are some key performance tips everyone can use right now, because success leaves clues for those willing to learn.

Let's take a quick look. To achieve success and become what I call a 'Possibility Seeker' you need:

- **Good coaching:** Someone who can help you pick up good habits fast so you don't have to undo bad habits slowly – like coach David Sturt ('Steggles')

- **Like-minded people:** A group of committed, passionate people who are heading in the same direction is a very powerful force, and will encourage you to achieve your goals more quickly than if you go it alone

- **To stretch yourself:** As the saying goes, 'if you're the best in your group then you're in the wrong group'

- **Accountability:** Someone or something that will hold you accountable for results

- **To take action:** Positive thinking is important, but positive *doing* through taking action will get you further, faster

- **Data:** Don't guess – analyse and assess whether you are on track or off track, what you need to improve and what you can celebrate

- **Discipline:** Getting out of bed at 5am to ride is not natural for most people, but it is necessary if you want to improve.

This book will also cover many aspects of business life. It will be relevant to you whether you are a business leader, entrepreneur, manager, employee working your way up or looking for your next opportunity. I have experienced all of these roles and will bring my experience to you as best I can.

I have one caveat: I am still on my journey, too. I am learning, changing and growing, and possess the very human trait of seeing the world not as it is, but as I think it is. But as a Possibility Seeker I am consistently curious, constantly evolving and open to new opportunities.

This book (unlike my previous books) has been written during the amazing era of social media, which means we can connect and talk about 'the Art of the Possible' so much more easily. Look me up via my Art of the Possible podcast and social media channels, and tell me your story. I want to know what great ideas and dreams you have, what you have done and what you are aiming for in the future on this journey called life, so that we can all improve and learn together.

Rob Hartnett
robhartnett.com
@robhartnett

PART I
GETTING
STARTED

'Greatness looks like madness until it finds context.'

Russell Brand

1. Preparing for possibility

'Impossible is just a big word thrown around by small men who find it easier to live in the world they've been given than to explore the power they have to change it.'

Muhammad Ali

Since childhood, I have believed in possibilities. At times when I have been in a dark place, as a teenager, an adult and a father with seemingly no way out, I have been able to change my mindset to get curious and search for another way.

Early in my working life, I was struck by the thought that there had to be something better in life. I was doing okay – I had an accounting degree, had worked for some great brands and was now in enterprise computer sales – but something was telling me there was more to achieve. I decided to take action, and thought I might find the answer in a bookstore. The problem was, I really didn't know what I was looking for. It wasn't a business book; it definitely wasn't a motorsport or sailing book, which were areas of the store I knew well. After a while, an assistant asked if he could help me. I admit I struggled for words. I recall saying something like, 'I am looking for a book or a resource to help me get better'. 'Get better at what?' he asked. After a bit of back-and-forth, he took me to the personal development section and pulled out Tony Robbins' book, *Awaken the Giant Within*. 'Have a go at this one', he said. 'It seems to be selling well.'

From that moment on I was hooked on personal development. I am forever grateful to that assistant for helping me out. A few years later, I met Tony and corresponded with him on a couple of business ideas, and it was also that book that inspired my world championship in sailing. (For those of you wondering: yes, I did walk on hot coals at one of Tony's 'Awaken the Giant' live sessions, and it was a mind-blowing experience.)

MY LIFE MANTRA

Around the time I found Tony Robbins I also developed my life mantra, and I have stayed true to it for 20 years. It might work for you, too (or you could develop your own):

1. **Live:** Participate in life; don't be a spectator.

2. **Love:** Give love and accept love.

3. **Laugh:** Have a sense of humour.

4. **Learn:** Always be open to learning from anyone.

5. **Legacy:** Give back. Coach others. Be a connector, not a climber.

Live

How good is living? By this, I mean really participating in life, not just watching everyone else do it. I know I live in Australia, and it's a pretty good place to be. However, suicide remains the leading cause of death for Australians aged between 15 and 44, and there are more than eight deaths by suicide in Australia each day.[1] This is something that astounds and saddens me, and that I hope this book might address.

Living is not about how much you have. Wealth is a measure of success for some people, but there are plenty of rich unhappy people. Someone once said to me, 'Given the choice I would rather cry in a Porsche than a Pontiac!'. I believe the reason you are crying is the critical question, when there is so much to be happy about. If you are crying because you can't really afford the Porsche, then sell it. Assets are fine to own, as long as they don't own you. I have sold several Porsches over the years to use my money in different ways. I admit there were times when I was with business colleagues who all had expensive cars that I thought to myself, 'Maybe I should have kept it'. One time, my host introduced me to the others by saying, 'This is Rob; he is between Porsches right now'. That was so empowering! Yes, there will be another one coming if that's what I want. Life is about swings and roundabouts, changing seasons and adjusting your sail to suit the wind. I don't believe assets should ever prevent you from living your life.

Very few of us know how long we have to live. Too many people, especially small business owners, put off going overseas or pursuing a dream assuming they will be as healthy and fit at 70 as they are at 40. It's not necessarily true. Take risks when your body and mind are in the right place to enjoy them. For example, my good friend Phil wanted to have a fast cruising yacht in Europe so he could spend the European summer on it. When he bought it he named it *Kids' Inheritance*. Nice work Phil. He does invite his kids to go cruising with him, though!

Bronnie Ware, an Australian palliative nurse and author of *The Top Five Regrets of the Dying*, recorded the biggest regrets of patients she worked with over a period of eight years. The number one regret from both men and women was this:

> *I wish I'd had the courage to live a life true to myself, not the life others expected of me.*

Bronnie explains:

> *When people realise that their life is almost over and look back clearly on it, it is easy to see how many dreams have gone unfulfilled. Most people had not honoured even a half of their dreams and had to die knowing that it was due to choices they had made, or not made.*[2]

Pursue your dreams and your goals. Don't bail out early. Be an inspiration for those around you – and that includes me, because I want to see you happy.

Love

A seminar audience member once asked me what I thought the most important thing in life was. I said love. Love comes in many forms: you can have love for a partner and love for your children. I have three boys with my wife Leisa. Sometimes we get asked if we have a favourite son. The question has always been strange to me. I have always felt an equal love for all three at all times. Trust me, they have tested my resolve on this but still the love is equal.

To give love though, you must first have it. The most import-ant love is the one you have for yourself. Later in the book, I talk about Lance Picioane, founder of the charity Love Me Love You. It's a perfect name for Lance's organisation, and it has to be in that order because you can't give what you don't have.

To be loved is another thing altogether. Stephen Colbert once asked Keanu Reeves what he thought happens when we die. Keanu replied: 'When it happens, the people who love us will miss us.' What a wonderful answer.

Laugh

Laughing is so important for your health and happiness. According to entrepreneur James Altucher, kids laugh around 300 times a day whereas adults only laugh five times a day. Life is simple; we grow up and make it complicated. Remember: you can be successful and still have fun. Three times road cycling world champion Peter Sagan has a saying: 'Why so serious?'. Peter is known for his antics and sense of humour, and also for his sprinting speed. Nice guys do win.

In 2005 I created a book called *What Marketing People Know about Sales*. On the back cover, it read 'What Sales People Know about Marketing'. The inside pages of the book were completely blank. It was a direct mail piece designed to raise awareness of the issues in having separate sales and marketing departments. The book ended being picked up by Brolga Publishing and dis-tributed by Penguin Books. I could not believe it when I saw it retailing in a major bookstore for $9.00! After we sold out the first print run I created a second edition, which included a bonus CD (blank, of course). I still discover people across the world who remember that book; the creative director of one of the world's largest advertising agencies even told me it cracked him up. You have to make your own fun; you never know where it might lead.

Don't take yourself so seriously; lighten up, laugh a little more. Having fun doesn't mean you need to be the life of the party or a stand-up comedian, but do open your eyes and ears and try to see the funny side. It will help you mentally and physically.

Learn

I always make an effort to connect with smart people who I can learn from. I had the pleasure of meeting Tony Robbins' mentor Jim Rohn on his Australia tour; I interviewed Brian Tracy for SkyNews with Robert Gottliebsen and, more recently, I spent time with Dr John C Maxwell, which led me to the Godfather of Influence Dr Robert Cialdini. All these people and many more have something you can learn. The internet gives you access to TED Talks, YouTube, Instagram and micro-learning programs from some of the most prestigious universities in the world. But you will only learn if you take action: people won't come to you.

I am constantly amazed by how few people in the audience at my speaking engagements say they have spent their own money on self-development. This is especially the case when I speak at large corporate organisations; hardly any hands go up. These people are clearly not good investors, because the best investment you will ever make is in yourself. Don't expect your employer, the government or your parents to provide you with all the learning opportunities. As Australian Football League legend Ron Barassi says, 'If it's to be, it's up to me'.

Legacy

What will you be remembered for? I believe that for the first part of our life we are building our résumé of awesomeness. After 50, I believe we build our legacy – by this I mean the nice things people say about us in our eulogy for example. However, you don't have to wait for 50 years – you can start building your legacy at any age. What are the things you really want to be remembered for?

Writing this book is a legacy. There are things in this book I hope will help people in many years to come. I will probably need to go back to it myself, too, from time to time. My legacy to my family is to build a cohesive unit of love and respect. I didn't have an especially close relationship with my father growing up and, for most of my adult life, it was respectful but not close. He didn't have a close relationship with his father either, from what I can tell, and I know he and his siblings do not have much of a relationship with each other either, which is a shame. These distant relationships seemed normal growing up: we never had family gatherings, and that was okay. However, with a family of your own, you start to take a different view. My legacy is to break a couple of generations of non-communication. So, my most important legacy is to raise my three boys to be men who love each other and will always be there for each other. I know my sister, Susan, is also passionate about raising her daughters in a spirit of friendship and connection with their cousins.

I am super lucky in this respect to have a mentor in this area in my wife, Leisa. Leisa comes from a large, loving family who always get together. Times may get tough, but they always have each others' back. I have been able to see my nephews and nieces grow up, and witness how well it can work. The good news is: if you are intentional about it, you can repair some of the earlier issues that were not yours as a child. Through the magic of social media, I am now more connected to my side of the family than ever. (This includes my Auntie Margie, who is a social media whiz in her late eighties – she's crushing Facebook and Messenger.)

ANYTHING IS POSSIBLE

I want to make a point early on about this book's title, *It's All Possible*. My intention is to provide you with a guide, using real examples, that illustrates not that *everything* is possible, but that *anything* is possible. You might not be able to achieve everything you have always wanted at the same time, but many dreams and goals are possible during your life if you have a big enough 'why'. Most importantly, you must take action and be intentional about achieving your goals. This won't happen all at once, but strategically over time.

I truly believe that it *is* all possible for you if you are intentional. The problem is, most people are not intentional. The leadership guru Dr John C Maxwell, who I am now proud to call a mentor, was challenged as a young leader with the question: 'John, how are you intentionally growing?'. When I read this question, it challenged me like I hope it is challenging you. I thought, 'Well, I want to grow; I believe I am growing; I learn from my mistakes; and I hope I am growing through my daily experiences. But, am I intentional about it?' Given that hope is not a strategy, I had to admit that, frankly, I was not intentional about my growth: I just assumed it would happen. Well, good luck with that strategy, Rob!

To intentionally grow you need the three Ds of intentionality:

1. **Desire:** You have to really want it.

2. **Discipline:** You have to be prepared to do the work.

3. **Determination:** You have to be prepared to push through when challenged.

Sound easy? It isn't. Worth it? From my experience, totally.

It's All Possible, the name for this book, came to me after doing some speaking engagements on the topic 'The Art of the Possible' to various leaders, entrepreneurs and businesspeople. So many of them, especially the Millennials, told me their leaders simply did not inspire them or encourage innovative and creative thinking. This made me sad, as I am passionate about possibility and giving people a chance to shine. It makes me think that most leaders are not leading: they are managing, keeping below the radar to survive the next restructure.

So why this book now? Because we need more Possibility Seekers who can become Possibility Leaders and adopt the Art of the Possible by asking 'How might we?' as opposed to 'Why would we?'. 'How might we?' is aspirational, inspirational, hopeful and positive. By asking 'Why would we?' you are being limiting, sticking to old beliefs, excuses and negativity.

INTRODUCING THE 4-STEP POSSIBILITY SYSTEM©

Throughout my business and sporting life, I have observed the habits, routines, visions, processes and skills of the world's best. I have always set my benchmark in line with the top achievers – no matter their gender, race, country or religion. I have studied the best in business, from corporate CEOs, entrepreneurs, faith leaders, salespeople, marketers and C-suite leaders. In sport, I have studied the best in motorsport, motorcycling, cycling, yachting, all codes of football, ice hockey and many others. More importantly, I have applied the principles these leaders endorse countless times, and I am doing so right now. My 4-Step Possibility System© has been designed so you can use it to live your purpose, crush your goals and achieve your aspirations. (By the way, feel free to improve it to suit your needs. I am just the son of a motor mechanic from Moonee Ponds, Australia who wants to see what is possible.)

The 4 Steps are as follows:

1. **Attitude and mindset:** Your *will* – your passion, resilience and desire

2. **Vision:** Your *why* – your dream, goal or purpose

3. **Strategy:** Your *what* – the keys to achieve your vision

4. **Action:** Your *how* – knowledge, process and skills

POSSIBILITY VERSUS TRUTH

'Possibility' is such a positive, uplifting word. It inspires hope, even when you are in a tight spot. It can make you feel empowered and like there is a way forward and a light ahead. What I like about possibility is that it's contrarian; it flies in the face of facts, or the truth as we currently see it. One of my mentors, entrepreneur Paul Martinelli, says 'Possibility is the flipside of truth'. It sounds controversial, doesn't it?

In Australia, we are seeing some positive changes in financial services and wealth management. Some people in these industries are clinging to facts, while others have embraced possibility.

I have clients on both sides. The key difference is the approach of their leaders.

One of my clients operates in the packaging business and manages two big accounts. One day, he met with his first key account and heard that its leadership team was nervous about the potential economic downturn (apparently economists have a pretty poor record in accurately forecasting recessions, by the way), so his client needed to halve its orders for branded packaging for the next six months. Later that day he visited his second key account. Walking into the meeting he sensed a similar theme, and sure enough, the marketing manager opened the meeting by saying, 'Our leadership team has seen an economic downturn on the horizon'. My client's shoulders slumped. However, he was quickly revived when the manager went on to say, 'Given this, we think it is a unique opportunity to gain market share as we can buy in-store advertising for the lowest cost we have seen, so we want to double our usual orders for the next six months'. Same city, same day, same market; the difference was in attitude and mindset.

Clinging to 'facts' can cause us to miss many great opportunities. Often, supposed 'truths' are backed up by research that proves to be incorrect when it is examined from a different angle or approached later with the benefits of time and technology. Sometimes all it takes is for people to move past their self-imposed limitations. Here are some examples:

Before the early 16th century, it was thought the sun and planets revolved around Earth. We now understand Earth and the planets orbit instead around the sun, thanks to the theories of Copernicus who challenged the prevailing theory of his time.

Until the 1950s, experts and evidence had shown humans could not run a mile faster than four minutes (this was disproven by Englishman Roger Bannister, who asked 'How might I?' and famously did it).

13

Speaking broadly, Isaac Newton's theories were superseded by Albert Einstein, who was then superseded by Stephen Hawking.

It was believed a monohulled yacht could not sail faster than 600 nautical miles in 24 hours (in 2015 my friend Ken Read and his crew on Comanche *did 618 nautical miles in 24 hours).*

In 2009 I competed in the World Masters Games in sailing, coming 6th overall in the Laser Radial Class. In 2017, I competed in the World Masters Games in Auckland in road cycling. If you had suggested to me in 2015 when I bought my first road bike that I would swap my lifejacket for lycra I would have laughed at you. But if it's possible for me, it's possible for you to shift gears too (pun intended!).

Am I saying that anyone can be anything they want if they just try hard enough and have a strategy? No. But I am saying that anyone can *be better* at what they want if they are willing to put in the time and effort it takes to do so. Certainly, there are physical and mental problems that can act as constraints, but many have shown that problems can be overcome with determination and perseverance:

Doug Flutie, star NFL quarterback, was told he was too short to play pro football.

Tom Dempsey, born without toes on his right foot and missing four fingers on his right hand, kicked the longest field goal in NFL history.

Quentin Kenihan was born with a rare bone disease and was confined to a wheelchair, yet he went on to star in his own TV show and in movies including Mad Max: Fury Road.

Ludwig van Beethoven overcame deafness and depression to become one of the world's greatest composers.

Bethany Hamilton lost her left arm in a shark attack and still became a national champion surfer in the US.

Jessica Cox, born without arms, flies planes, drives cars, and holds a black belt in taekwondo.

Be very cautious about setting limits on people – including yourself.

THE POSSIBILITY ZONES©

The Possibility Zones© is a tool I created that gives you a visual representation of how far you are currently pushing yourself, and where you could be if you adopt my 4-Step Possibility System©. The size of the circles represents the energy and effort you put in to achieving your goals. Take a look now and write down which zone you are currently in, which zone you have operated in previously, and which zone you would like to be in within the next two years.

The Possibility Zones©

	COMFORT ZONE		GROWING ZONE		POSSIBILITY ZONE	
	1	2	3	4	5	6
What I ...	Do now	Could do but don't	Could learn to do	Could do with will and skill	Believe is possible for other people	**What is actually possible for me!**

The further you progress through the zones, the more uncomfortable you might feel – but with each zone you reach, you are getting closer to what is really possible for you if you follow the 4-Step Possibility System©. In truth, most of us only aspire to Zone 3 when we should be reaching Zone 6. I am telling you it is possible – I have done it myself, and I know you can, too. I can also tell you a secret. The right team can help you get to Zone 6 faster!

BELIEVE IN THE POWER OF POSSIBILITY

In his book *Mentors*, Russell Brand outlines the 12 Steps he took to break his drug addiction. The first three are:

1. Admit you have a problem
2. Believe in the possibility of change
3. Ask for help and follow suggestions.

The second one is vital. We must genuinely believe in the possibility of something better, and we need to see and experience the possibilities that are open to us – even if it is only through visualisation. I still find this part hard, and it takes real concentration, focus and intentionality to seek out the possible. I know it can be done, and so do you. How many times have you heard yourself or someone else say, 'I didn't think that was possible, yet I have achieved it'? I am told drug rehabilitation programs that are run by people with lived experience of addiction are much more successful, because it is much easier to believe in possibility when you see someone like you achieve success.

That is the underlying reason I wrote this book. I am not a celebrity, I don't have superpowers and I am not from a wealthy background. I am a dad from the suburbs in Australia having a go and seeing what is possible.

If you're a parent, you only need to look at your kids to see the power of possibility. When my boys started high school we attended an event at which the principal made a point of speaking to the eager parents gathered in anticipation. He said:

> *I know you are keen for your little treasures to become lawyers, doctors, engineers or accountants, or to work in other roles you value highly. We understand this. But you need to know this: when your children leave this place of learning, they will most likely go on to study courses that have not yet been designed, to prepare them for jobs that don't yet exist. Our role is to uncover the passions in your children and have them pursue these, and prepare them for the pathway to whatever career they may choose. Your role is to keep paying the fees on time and ensure the homework is done.*

Our children must be taught the power of possibility, too, because anything is possible in the future. What do you think is possible for them, for the rest of your family, for your business, for your friends, and for yourself? The world is a big place, and opportunities abound for you.

Meet Tyler Bevins, professional gamer

Tyler Bevins, better known by his screen name Ninja, is a professional gamer, YouTuber and Twitch streamer. As of May 2019, he is the most-followed streamer on live streaming platform Twitch, with more than 14 million followers and an average of 40 000-plus viewers per week. He makes around $500 000 per month just from Twitch. When you add to this his YouTube advertising revenue, endorsements and sponsorships, he is earning around US$1.5 to US$2 million per month! Tyler has since moved to Microsoft's streaming platform Mixer on which he amassed over 1 million subscribers in less than a week. In the Possibility Zones, Tyler is operating in Zone 5 and is looking towards what is possible in Zone 6.

2. Preparing
for change

'Until you make the unconscious conscious,
it will direct your life and you will call it fate.'

Carl Jung

There are plenty of fallacies regarding change. One of the most commonly cited myths is that it takes 21 days to change a habit. If we do a little myth busting, we can trace the origins of this statement to a 1950s plastic surgeon named Maxwell Maltz. Maltz noticed that when he performed an operation, his patients would take around 21 days to adjust to the change in their bodies. In his book *Psycho-Cybernetics*, he wrote: 'It requires a minimum of about 21 days for an old mental image to dissolve and a new one to jell'. (Note the important words: 'minimum' and 'about'!) As Maltz's statement was recited over many years it was eventually believed to be scientific fact that it takes exactly 21 days to change a habit.

Enter University College London researcher, Dr Phillippa Lally. Determined to test how long it actually takes us to form or change a habit, Dr Lally discovered it actually takes between 18 and 254 days, with the average being 66 days.[3] So, don't be disheartened if change takes longer than you expect. Look for evolution not revolution in your life if you want to change. The reality is that most people overestimate what they can do in a year and underestimate what they can do in five years.

MANAGING YOUR THOUGHTS

Researchers have yet to prove exactly how many thoughts we have per day, but one thing is clear: it numbers in the many thousands. We are constantly generating thoughts and ideas, often without even noticing. Have you ever found that when you are in a quiet place free from distractions, such as in an aeroplane or the shower, you seem to have more thoughts?

Feelings drive thoughts

According to Dr David Hawkins, author of *Letting Go: The Pathway of Surrender*, it is the accumulated pressure of feelings that causes thoughts. One feeling, for instance, can create thousands of thoughts over time. If we could surrender to the underlying painful feeling, all of those thoughts would disappear instantly. The great value of knowing how to surrender is that any and all feelings can be let go of at any time and any place in an instant, and it can be done continuously and effortlessly.

You have the power to choose your thoughts, just like you can choose your radio station or favourite podcast. One night, we were driving home to Melbourne from a Queensland sailing regatta with the boys' boats on the trailer bouncing along the highway. We were deep in the country without much in the way of radio signals. We could have put on a familiar music track, but Ben, my eldest son, suggested we listen to digital radio through his phone. Suddenly we had more stations than we could cope with. Your thoughts are like a digital radio platform. There is always a broadcast going on, but you can choose which channel you listen to. We also need to be aware that our mind might have its own station preferences, so we need to make a conscious effort to only tune in to what we want to hear.

Repetitive thoughts

Joe Dispenza, author of *You Are the Placebo: Making Your Mind Matter*, says that 90 per cent of the thoughts we have are exactly the same ones we had the day before. Deepak Chopra, the prolific speaker and writer, agrees with this. This is key to why people find it hard to change, especially if they continue to associate with the same people and keep the same routines and habits.

I worked part-time as a motor mechanic for my father from a young age. It was a good, profitable business, and my father was a first-class engineer. Our clients were mostly European and British sports and luxury car owners, and we had some great cars to work on. At around age 17, I mentioned to my father that there was another garage business and service station coming up for sale in the area, and suggested we look at expanding. His reply floored me, but in hindsight it was totally consistent. He said: 'Are you kidding? If we buy another business that will mean more bloody customers, and I have enough trouble with the ones we have now.' Later on, we started to have some fleet cars come to us. I suggested we pitch to some big companies around our area for all their fleet work. His reply? 'Fleet work? We would be too busy, and they don't pay well.'

My father seemed to be dogged by negativity, mainly because his thoughts never changed. I once asked him to watch the final lap of Bathurst with me on TV. As Peter Brock climbed the mountain for the final time with his Holden Torana SLR5000 purring in perfect form, my father couldn't help himself. He looked at the TV and said, 'In my experience, engines are at their best just before they blow up'. Thankfully, Peter 'Perfect' Brock's car was in great form, had new tyres and was low on fuel, allowing him to complete a flawless final lap and take the victory. 'Gee, Brocky was lucky today', my father said.

Even today, when I call my parents, just before my father says 'I will get your mother' (apparently this is a pretty common phrase for men of his generation) he asks how I am. I will reply something like, 'Great, going well, wonderful', and he will always say, 'You're lucky, things are bad around here'.

I am sure you know people like this. Like me, you may even be related to one. I recently heard Gary Vaynerchuk talking about one of his grandmothers. Gary said that, growing up, when all the kids were laughing she would say, 'If there is too much laughing in the house you know crying is next'.[4] He thought nothing of it back then, but now, as a parent himself, he knows it makes no sense. People who fall prey to repetitive thoughts don't mean any harm; they just see the world in a particular way, and their thoughts reinforce that.

Negative thoughts

American motivational speaker and author Les Brown believes around 80 of our thoughts are negative. It's not just you – it's all of us. This means we must fight hard to find the positive thoughts, and why positive self-talk is so vital a strategy to have. If you are sceptical about this, let me ask you the following questions:

- As you planned your week, did you allocate an hour or so to stress out – or does that happen naturally?

- Do you put aside time each week to go through your regrets – or does that happen naturally?

In her book *Grit: The Power of Passion and Perseverance*, Angela Duckworth says that one of the key ways to change our outlook is to use optimistic self-talk. You can feed yourself with positivity by listening to a podcast, reading inspirational quotes on Instagram, reading a book (hopefully like this one) and working with positive people. Whatever it is, you need to be intentional about it.

Negative self-talk can really take hold and get out of control. One way I have found to combat the negative voice in my head is to recognise it for what it is: not me, but a negative voice. To differentiate the negative voice from myself (as in Rob, the handsome positive one!), I call my negative voice Richard – or Dick, for short. The reason I like this name is that some of the time Richard can be quite helpful, like when he reminds me to wear a helmet when cycling or to look out for bad driving on the road that might affect me. But often Richard can be a real Dick. This is when he suggests the worst possible outcome or drags me off with him to his favourite city, Negative Town. (Dick's version of Negative Town is so popular it has its own hotels and Airbnb options, as he often likes to stay a while!)

I have developed some strategies for myself when I suspect Richard is being a Dick:

- Is this thought helping or hindering me? (Helping = Richard, hindering = Dick.)

- Is this thought protecting me or harming me? (Protecting = Richard, harming = Dick.)

- Is this thought based on facts or assumption? (Facts = Richard, assumptions = Dick.)

When I run these filters I find it gives me clarity. You can do them very quickly – actually, you have to, given the number of thoughts we have each day.

I also balance things out with my other voice: the voice of positive thoughts, organisational support, reminders and general helpfulness. I call this voice Jock. The inspiration for Jock came from the character of the same name in the movie *Mortdecai*. The namesake of the movie, Mortdecai, introduced Jock as his man servant and protector, helpful for when things get a 'little sticky'. Jock always had Mortdecai's back and would keep him organised and on track.

Jock balances out Richard when Richard's being a Dick.

Rachel Hollis, *New York Times* best-selling author of *Girl, Stop Apologizing*, says that women are often afraid of themselves. She believes women are constantly apologising for who they are and what they want out of life, and for the time to pursue both. I often hear women putting themselves down and underestimating themselves. But it doesn't need to be this way! My beautiful wife, Leisa, never wanted to date a boy with a sports car – she wanted one for herself! This was not an easy task for her. Growing up, Leisa was the youngest child by a long way, so her siblings had grown up and had families of their own by the time she was learning to drive. Leisa's father had also unexpectedly passed away when she was just 16. With the support of her mother, she embarked on buying her dream car: a red MGB, the iconic British sports car. She had plenty of friends tell her how it wasn't a good idea; that MGBs were unreliable, cold in winter and expensive to maintain – and what about the lack of rear seats for children? But she pursued her dream. One day I saw Leisa driving her MGB – well, actually, I heard her first: she had a performance exhaust system that I could hear from 2km away. She drove past me, parked and got out of the car – blonde hair flowing. We met properly a few months after this and have been married now for 27 years.

Julie Bishop is one of the most powerful women in Australia. When asked how she maintains her business savvy she said: 'Do not let others define who you are and what you can achieve. Set your own standards, set your own benchmarks, and make them high'.[5] I think that's sound advice from someone who has achieved so much in a male-dominated environment.

BUILDING YOUR SELF-IMAGE

If your self-image is not in harmony with where you want to go and who you want to be, then change or achievement is going to be very difficult. When you cling to thoughts such as 'I can't, it won't' you will always find evidence to support your negative view.

Our view of the world is formed not by how it is but *how we see it*. We are constantly analysing the world, often through our subconscious mind. I believe our subconscious thoughts are formed by what I call HBOE:

H   Habits
B   Beliefs
O   Opinions
E   Experiences.

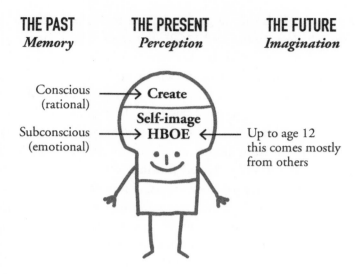

THE PAST
Memory

THE PRESENT
Perception

THE FUTURE
Imagination

Conscious
(rational)

→ Create

Self-image
HBOE

Subconscious
(emotional)

Up to age 12
this comes mostly
from others

Much of our HBOE is formed by the messages we receive from other people – especially our parents and guardians, when we are younger. In the movie *Talladega Nights*, fictional NASCAR legend Ricky Bobby always believed that if you weren't first in a race, you were last. He lived his whole life believing this because that's what his father had told him as a child. When he challenged his father as an adult, his father could barely remember saying it – and when he did recall, he said, 'Wow, Ricky, that doesn't make any sense at all. You could be second, you could be third, fourth, hell, you could be fifth!'.

In his book *Letting Go: The Pathway of Surrender*, Dr David Hawkins explains that part of us is attached to the familiar, no matter how painful or inefficient it is. It may seem bizarre, but part of us actually enjoys an impoverished life and all the negativity that goes with it.[6]

Are we willing to imagine a new life for ourselves, character-ised by effortless success, freedom from resentment, gratitude for all that's happened to us, inspiration, love, joy, win-win resolu-tions, happiness and creative expression?

One of the biggest hurdles to happiness, Hawkins tells us, is the belief that it isn't possible: 'There's got to be a catch'; 'It's too good to be true'; 'It can happen for others but not for me.' But the reality is that it *is* possible and that's good news for us all.

In his speech to the 2014 graduating class at Maharishi University of Management, actor Jim Carrey said that while our eyes can observe information that can assist our learning, our subconscious mind also uses our eyes as projectors to find evi-dence of what we believe is the truth, according to the image we have formed of ourselves (via HBOEs).

I have always had a natural curiosity to understand what drives people and how and why they have achieved things in their life. I have also been gifted with communication skills that allow me to communicate easily and ask questions. But this talent remained hidden for many years. Growing up, I was shy, introverted and brought up in a traditional family setting wherein children should be spoken to and not heard from. My world was one where 'loose lips sink ships' and where talking was not seen as displaying good manners. These are some of the belief systems I have had to work through in my quest to seek out the possible. I didn't realise I had a talent for communication until I started my working career at KPMG. It was there that I began to be influenced by new HBOEs from outside my family circle.

When I was younger and considering what I wanted to do as a career I thought to myself: 'I'm going to go into real estate. I like property, design and development'. But my parents said: 'That's too dangerous. You will have to start out collecting rent from criminals and low lifes, and you might get stabbed'. So, I thought on it more and came up with the idea of studying law. My parents' response was: 'You don't want to do that. You'll be working with the criminals who couldn't pay their rent'.

Next, I turned my mind to a more creative pursuit: 'I'm thinking about TV and film production'. My parents' response? 'All those people are off the planet and mostly on substances they buy from the criminals.' (The same ones, presumably, who don't pay lawyers and go around stabbing real estate agents!)

Despite their great advice, I went my own way and landed a role in finance at mining giant Rio Tinto. In my first month, I was given access to one of their very expensive portable PCs from Compaq (remember them?). I took it home to do some additional spreadsheet work. My father saw the PC and said, 'I thought you were an accountant. What have they got you doing, playing computer games? Those things won't teach you about business'.

Take some time now and think about the values, principles and beliefs you might have inherited from others during your earlier years. Do they still serve you? What beliefs do you still carry that are past their expiry date?

A note for parents

If you are a parent, you may also want to think about the HBOEs you are introducing to your children and whether these might be limiting their chances of becoming Possibility Seekers.

My wife and I were very critical of our eldest son when he was in his mid-teens, particularly in regards to his mobile phone use. He was constantly on it, much to our frustration – especially at the dinner table. However, what we missed was that he was quietly building a significant following on Instagram and YouTube, honing his natural skills as a videographer and filmmaker and building a global audience at the same time. As I write this, he has built several Instagram channels to tens of thousands of followers, and his Hartnett Media YouTube channel is on its way to 200 000 subscribers. Once my wife and I saw that he was receiving Google advertising revenue from this work, we understood what this venture meant to him and immediately changed our belief systems. Now we insist he spends more time on his phone!

THE POWER OF THE SUBCONSCIOUS MIND

How exciting is this: once you understand how the mind works there is no stopping you from inputting what you want in the future into your mind. The subconscious mind can't differentiate between what is real and what is imagined. It stands to reason, then, that we can start achieving possibilities by defining what we want, and then bringing it to life in our mind through imagination. You might be wondering, why doesn't everyone do this if it's so easy? The simple answer, I believe, is that most people don't take the time to work out exactly what they want. They mostly focus on what they *don't* want and, unsurprisingly, keep on getting more of that. You need to focus; by that I mean you must really define what you want in minute detail, and then visualise and actually *feel* what it's like having it. Here are some examples of what you could imagine:

- I am a successful business owner

- Money comes easily to me

- I have an amazing four-bedroom house in the location I choose

- I have a wonderful marriage

- I am fit and healthy

- The answers to the exam came easily to me.

Select one or two of these that are relevant or – preferably – come up with your own. Now, what does it feel like having what you want right now, in the present tense?

When Leisa and I decided to move house to be closer to the beach this was a big step for us. In the beginning, we were not crystal clear on where and what the next house would look like. Rather than leaving such a big decision to chance we decided to use the power of the subconscious to make the goal real. We did this by:

- Visiting cafés and shops in our preferred locations often, as if we were already living there

- Going to auctions and house inspections

- Sailing our sailboats at local clubs in the area

- Visiting friends who already lived in the area.

Then we took two important steps: we wrote down in detail what our dream house would be like, in as much detail as possible; and we made a public commitment to the plan by telling people we were moving, even though we were still a couple of years away from the actual move. (We did this so these people would keep us accountable.)

Yes, this all took time and yes, our boys often complained about driving to the beachside suburbs for coffee and shopping when there were closer options. But the work paid off: we were able to sell our current house on Christmas Eve, and purchase a new one in our chosen location on New Year's Eve.

However, the real shock came to me while packing up for our move, and I found a journal from two years back that I had not looked at since. It contained the description of the house Leisa and I wanted to buy and its location that I had written. It was identical to the property we were moving into. I was blown away. I had heard people talk about this happening and now I had witnessed it first-hand. Our imagination can be a very powerful tool if we let it do its job.

What about feelings?

Feelings are tremendously underrated. They are the easiest way to get in touch with what you really want, and have the full experience of imagining what it will be like when you achieve your dreams. If you are struggling to imagine the feeling, why not try out your dream in real life, and pay attention to the feelings that come up? I call this 'renting your dream'. If you want to move to a new country or a new town, go and stay there for a short time to immerse yourself in the place. If you want to buy a sports car, hire one for a weekend. If you want to travel the world, take a small trip. I guarantee that if your dream is truly for you, the feelings you get when you experience it on a small scale will make you even more determined to make your dream happen. The reason this works is that you were specific: your five senses experienced exactly what it will be like when your dreams come true.

PASSION WILL KEEP YOU GOING

Now, I know some of you may still not be clear on what you want. A way of getting some clarity is to start with something you are passionate about. Passion is a vital ingredient in any change process, because change will inevitably become difficult at some point – especially if you need to influence others who are invested in keeping things as they are!

Passion will get you through when the going gets tough. It will be the reason you get up early, work late, travel further and put in more. You won't have success in anything without passion.

31

Here are three questions that I find useful when uncovering a passion:

- What really fires you up?
- What keeps you up at night?
- What activities make you feel like time disappears?

If you still can't find something you are passionate about, you might like to work through the following goal areas and see if there is anything within these categories you feel motivated to achieve:

- Career
- Lifestyle
- Contribution
- Hobbies
- Legacy.

If you can harness your passion, you will be well on your way to achieving your goals and have a little power up your sleeve when the going gets tough.

PART II
THE FOUR-STEP POSSIBILITY SYSTEM©

'Men are disturbed not by things,
but by the views which they take of things.'

Epictetus

3. Step 1: Getting your attitude and mindset right

'Happiness is a state of mind in which our thinking is pleasant a good share of the time.'

Dr John A Schindler

The first step in my 4-Step Possibility System© is attitude and mindset. The state of your mind is the first thing you need to get sorted – the right attitude will set you up to power through any roadblocks and move more quickly towards the possible.

Wouldn't we all like to be happy? The quote on the previous page by Dr John A Schindler describes happiness from a medical standpoint. I really like it, because it doesn't put unreasonable demands on us. Russian psychologist K Kekcheyev found that when we think pleasant thoughts, we can see, taste, smell and hear better. Other research has backed up the link between improved eyesight and thinking pleasant thoughts. What's not to love?

DEVELOPING A POSITIVE ATTITUDE

I try to maintain a positive attitude, but find I have to work hard at it. One of the bonuses of valuing people and always believing I can learn from anyone is that I seem to get a lot of opportunities to meet amazing people. Not always famous or well known, but inspirational nonetheless. What they all have in common is a positive attitude to life, and this demonstrates that no matter who you are, a positive attitude makes it all possible for you.

Let's meet some of the people who are positive role models for me.

Dr Hannah MacDougall

> 'Ride with a smile, ride with purpose,
> ride in the moment.'

Dr Hannah MacDougall

Quite simply, Dr Hannah MacDougall is the most positive person I know. Her positive attitude, sense of gratitude and upbeat demeanour is infectious and inspirational. Many a time I have been cycling at 6.00am in the dark and cold towards the end of a training ride when all that is keeping me going is thinking about just how good coffee is, when Hannah will fly past yelling 'Woohoo!'. The way Hannah does it takes you back to the very first time you learned how to ride and discovered the freedom that a bike can give you.

But let's understand Hannah some more. Hannah has only one leg, and uses a prosthetic on the missing leg, which she was born without. Hannah is a dual Paralympian and previous world record holder, has captained the Australian swimming team at both the world championships and Paralympic Games, and completed a PhD in athlete wellbeing. Hannah is one of Australia's highest-performing para-athletes and competes at the elite level globally and is a member of the Victorian Institute of Sport. I cycle with her coach Nick Owen, who says Hannah is wonderful to coach: she sees everything as worth trying and always does it with a smile and sense of adventure. Hannah tells me she thinks she drives Nick mad with all her questions and pursuit of possibility.

Hannah once told me that negative thoughts stick like velcro if we let them, whereas positive thoughts are like Teflon – slippery and easy to fall away. She says we need to reverse that, making our positive thoughts like velcro. This is something she is very, very intentional about. She does this through mindfulness, plenty of sleep, meditation and working hard on her mindset every day. Hannah says she has trained all her friends and family to understand that at 9.01pm she turns into a pumpkin; given that a sleep-in for her is 6.00am, this makes perfect sense. What about you? If you want to join the 5.00am Club that so many people talk about, you need to start by going to bed about 90 minutes earlier than you are now. Understanding your sleep requirements is the first step, and then doing something about it with discipline is the second step.

I asked Hannah why she changed sport from swimming to cycling. She said it was all about passion. She just lost the passion for swimming after looking at the black line at the bottom of the pool for so many years, and being indoors became tiresome. Cycling gave her the outdoors and an always varying white line to get passionate about. Passion is key for longevity in sport. It was the main reason why I moved from sailing to cycling. I still love sailing, but I am not as passionate about it as I once was and that's okay. Hannah still goes for a swim and goes to the beach. It is not as though you need to walk away completely from a previous passion.

Lance Picioane

Lance Picioane, like Hannah MacDougall, is a force of positive energy. I met Lance through his role as an official partner of the Knights of Suburbia cycling group – a community organisation that aims to change the culture around mental health. (By the way, Lance is not a cyclist – in all honesty, his arms are the size of my legs. In fact, when he is asked to speak at cycling events he is banned from wearing singlets – it's just too embarrassing for the rest of us!)

At the peak of his career as an Australian Football League (AFL) footballer, Lance was on top of the world. He had a successful junior AFL career, captaining the Victorian AFL team to a premiership. He played at North Melbourne, Adelaide and eventually finished his career at Hawthorn. But during this time, he was living with demons – suffering from depression and anxiety as a teenager, and during his time as a player. Like so many young adults, Lance chose not to ask for help, but instead turned to partying and substance abuse.

By being truthful to himself, his family and his friends, Lance turned a corner and sought help. Although he still has his down days, Lance now lives a life full of love and happiness. In 2013, he fulfilled his dream of establishing the Love Me Love You Foundation to help young adults take control of their mental wellbeing and to live happier, more fulfilling lives. This was just 2.5 years after attempting suicide. To kick things off he walked from Sydney to Melbourne to raise awareness for the cause. His March with Me wellness walks are now run annually. Other Love Me Love You programs are based on Lance's experiences and aim to educate young adults about the importance of mental health, empowering them to 'Get Back to School, Back to Sport, Back to Life!'.

His vision today is to foster positive change through awareness, education and acceptance to help remove the stigma associated with mental health, drugs, alcohol, eating disorders and life hardships.

Carey Lohrenz

We have all seen the movie *Top Gun*, and witnessed the incredible efforts that are required to qualify at Top Gun Aviation School.

Carey Lohrenz was the first female F-14 Tomcat pilot to qualify as a Top Gun pilot, making her a pioneer in military aviation. Having flown missions worldwide as a combat mission-ready United States navy pilot, Carey is used to working in fast-moving, dynamic environments where inconsistent execution can generate catastrophic results. I met Carey in San Diego a few years ago and we connected as both my parents are pilots and my mother was a secretary in the Australian Women Pilots' Association. A point Carey made to me was this: a positive attitude does not guarantee success, but it will provide better options for success than a negative attitude. So true, and from someone that has achieved what Carey has in a very male-dominated environment I believe it.

Lee 'Hollywood' Turner

Lee Turner is a footballer turned cyclist. Lee is always on! If he knows you and sees you in a group he will shout out to you at the top of his lungs. I really enjoy riding with Lee (whenever I catch him) – it is always entertaining. I recall riding with Lee down the famous Beach Road in Melbourne and as we went past a house at some ungodly hour in the morning Lee yelled out at the top of his voice for the occupant, a cycling friend of his, to get out of bed and hit the road.

When I was building my Instagram account (@robhartnett) I, like many of you I'm sure, was often unsure of what to highlight and what people would like. Lee was riding with me one day and said, 'You know, I like your Insta mate. It's always positive. There is some really negative stuff on social, and it can get you down, but yours inspires me'. It's all I needed to hear. (You should definitely follow Lee's – he does it well. Check out @_leeturner.)

Because of his personality, attitude and thorough research he is often called upon to MC or lead cycling group rides. Lee has motivated me many times by encouraging me to give it all in a sprint to the finish or if he's out in a group, he'll encourage whoever is leading to push even harder. He also wears the most outrageous cycling gear (kit) of his cycling heroes.

I hope this section has inspired you. Who do you know that is a ball of positivity? How can you become more like them?

GET WORDS WORKING FOR YOU

This week, two good friends of mine lost their jobs. Both were in senior executive roles, had high credibility and I trust them implicitly. But words make a big difference in how they explained their situations:

Executive 1:   *'I was made redundant this week'.*

Executive 2:   *'There have been some structural changes in the business this week, and my role is impacted'.*

Executive 1's statement feels really personal. It's as if my friend himself became superfluous, rather than just his role at work. His words sounded so harsh and negative.

Executive 2's statement, on the other hand, is far less personal. By putting the emphasis on his role, my friend was able to communicate that while his job is impacted (and that clearly impacts him), it is more about a structural change in the business than a reflection of him personally. Who would you hire if you were interviewing these two and they described why they left their last role?

A big game changer for me was realising I could change my vocabulary from 'I have to do this' to 'I get to do this'. This simple shift in words has the power to change your view of life, and can help you to feel more gratitude for your situation. So many people in life don't get to do what most of us take for granted. A recent time when this thinking helped me was when I was writing this book. One day I found myself thinking, 'I have so much on right now, and on top of it I have to write two chapters this week'. I deliberately changed my thinking to, 'I *get* to write two chapters this week', and the task shifted immediately from a burden to a privilege.

When I work with people on their influencing skills, I ask them to think about what they want *for* the person they are trying to influence, rather than what they want *from* them. This approach works whether you would like a colleague to do something, want a customer to buy from you, or even if you want your child to change their behaviour. Focusing on what you want *for* that person means you need to get clear about the value in the request for the person you are trying to influence. It also helps you persevere when you understand that the change you are suggesting will be right for the person (and not just you) in the long term, while they may be resisting it in the short term.

I can't help thinking of a friend of mine, who never gets upset when the traffic lights turn red. He started calling them 'go lights' rather than 'stop lights', and it totally transformed his perception. The tactic of changing your perspective through language might seem trivial, but it really does work. If you're feeling sceptical, maybe you have a fixed mindset about how language can change your state?

Power words

Think about the words you use in your everyday conversations: in your emails, your message apps, your phone calls and face-to-face. Which side of the spectrum do the words you use most often fall into?

Power words	Powerless words
Yes	No
Opportunity	Challenge
Free	Can't
New	Opinion
You	Costly
Good	Expensive
Great	Later
Love	Waste
Growth	Not
Commitment	Bad
Guidance	Hate
Advice	Delay
Positive	Busy
Innovative	Bad
Proven	Just
Now	Slow
Exclusive	Negative
Benefit	Hard
Upside	Costly
Help	Sad
Benchmark	Don't
	Poor

This is not an exhaustive list, and you should consider building your own. Some of my clients use their list of words on posters or embedded in tools they use such as coaching templates to remind them to use power words when communicating. Even putting your list of power words in your phone's notes app can work to embed a change.

POSITIVE PHYSIOLOGY

How do you carry yourself? Do you stand up straight and walk tall and proud, or do you slump and schlep around? Good posture says so much about your confidence and demeanour. Do you greet people with a genuine smile or a forced expression?

I once had the privilege of taking a corporate speaking course at the National Institute of Dramatic Arts (NIDA). During the course, one of the elder statesmen of the acting world taught us to walk. Yes, at the age of 35, I was taught to properly walk! One of the tactics he taught me was to imagine I had a rod that travelled up my spine and continued through my neck and out through my head. Once I imagined this, I felt a metre taller. It was a revelation for someone like me – I always seemed to be in a hurry and had, over time, begun to constantly lean forward, somehow thinking I would get places faster. (All it did was give me bad posture.)

A few years back I had a speaking engagement in beautiful Bali. After doing a workout at the resort's gym I wanted to have a shower before my speaking gig, however the hot water in my room wasn't working properly. I had left several calls with reception, but no-one had shown up. I decided to head down to reception to sort the issue out. You can no doubt imagine my physiology: quick paced, focused and determined to get a result. As I approached the reception area one of the immaculately dressed staff stood up from the reception area, walked over and greeted me in the traditional Balinese way with her hands together as if to pray. She nodded and asked how she could assist. I was so disarmed by her greeting I literally had nothing to say.

Positive physiology is a tool of influence. Never underestimate its power.

CHOOSE A GROWTH MINDSET

'When you believe in yourself, you succeed better.
Hours spent questioning, doubting, fearing,
can be given over to working, exploring, living.'

Jennifer Lee

In her landmark book *Mindset: The New Psychology of Success*, Carol Dweck explored the concept of the growth mindset, fixed mindset and mixed mindset. In a fixed mindset, Dweck says, people believe their basic qualities, such as intelligence or talent, are fixed traits. Whereas with a growth mindset, people believe their ability can be developed through dedication and hard work. While Carol's work initially focused on mindset in relation to the education system, the connection to personal development, winning teams and leadership in business was an obvious extension.

I am a growth mindset person. This doesn't mean I have a growth mindset 100 per cent of the time – I do fall back into a fixed mindset from time to time, or find myself having a fixed mindset about certain things or even people. What a growth mindset does, though, is catch me in those moments – and the little voice in my head (Jock, not Richard – see chapter 2) will say, 'That sounds a bit like a fixed mindset'.

My growth mindset has allowed me to expand the Hartnett Group to contain four brands, each in an area I am passionate about:

- Hartnett Advisory – Leadership and change management
- Hartnett Media – Videography and photography, managed by my eldest son Ben
- Hartnett Film – Filmmaking, led by my middle son Finn
- Sailing Shack – Online classifieds and media for sailors.

I quite enjoy moving between these brands in my daily work, and many times they cross over. For example, we have done work for organisations that leveraged Hartnett Advisory, Hartnett Media and Sailing Shack.

In all of these endeavours I have applied my 4-Step Possibility System© and accelerated this with a growth mindset strategy:

- Having a goal (a dream with a date)

- Utilising best-practice coaches and mentors

- Not being afraid to fail

- Learning through every experience

- Leveraging previous connections and networks

- Always being grateful for the opportunity to live in a country that allows the freedom to pursue your passions.

I use the growth mindset in sport, too. When I was learning to climb hills on my bike, I dreaded hills at first. I couldn't go as fast as everyone else, I wasn't good at it and I only persevered because I love flying down the other side. At one event I was talking to another rider, and he said to me: 'I just race the flat circuits. I can't do hills, so I don't'. I immediately wondered, 'Do I sound like that?'. But that's not actually how I felt; my view was 'I can't do hills *yet*'. The power of that little word, 'yet', is so incredible. Once I found the word 'yet' I moved into a mixed mindset, and decided I could be better at hills if I got some coaching, checked my bike against other bikes and invested in hills training. Once I opened myself up to possibility, the options opened up for me.

Dweck says that if we approach them with a growth mindset, challenges are exciting rather than threatening. So rather than thinking, 'Oh, I'm going to reveal my weaknesses', you say, 'Wow, here's a chance to grow'. If you find yourself afraid of challenges, get yourself into a growth mindset, and think about all the growth potential that's possible if you follow this opportunity – even if it is out of your comfort zone. This is what happened to me with my hill climbing. I am still a long way from where I want to be, but I now have a plan and I know what is possible even as a master division rider coming into the sport later than most.

If you react to a setback defensively, wanting to hide it and make up excuses for it, you're in a fixed mindset. Instead, ask, 'What can I learn from this experience that can help me go forward next time?'. In a fixed mindset, you're so focused on the outcome. 'Will I look good? Will I live up to my reputation?' But in a growth mindset, you're focused on the process. Specifically, you must focus on the process that you need to engage in to bring about your success, as well as thinking about the processes you have previously engaged in that weren't so successful – and how you can learn from them next time.

While this all sounds logical and like common sense, it is amazing how many things that make sense never quite make it to common practice. You need to be intentional to reap the benefits.

BUILD YOUR RESILIENCE

'No retreat, no surrender.'

Bruce Springsteen

Resilience is the ability to cope when things go wrong; to bounce back after difficult times, and deal with challenges while holding your head high.

Clinical psychologist Andrew Fuller helps students (and parents!) develop coping skills during their final years of secondary school. He believes resilience is key to having a challenging but ultimately successful school experience. Developing a resilient mindset can help you to reduce anxiety and avoidant behaviour, ultimately assisting you to move forward and achieve your goals.

One day I was on the water supporting my son Ben in a yacht race and had observed Olympian Tom Burton start a race in shifty winds. To be honest, it did not look great for Tom at the beginning of the race, so I was keen to see if he recovered. I caught up with him onshore and it turns out not only did he recover, but he actually won! He said: 'It wasn't a great start – the wind shifted and left me back in the pack. So I aimed to get into the top 20 by the first rounding mark, and the top 10 by the end of the first lap. By the beginning of the last leg, I managed to get to fifth place'.

The secret to Tom's approach was, firstly, to avoid panicking, and secondly, to be realistic about the situation and what could be done. Tom assessed the situation with his logical head, not his emotional head. He broke down the problem and decided that given his speed, skills and abilities it was realistic for him to get back to the top 20 (of 60 sailors) by the first rounding mark. Once that was achieved, he re-assessed and selected his next goal. He also knew that the wind was shifty and if it had affected him badly there was every chance it would affect his competitors at some point, too. There was no point blaming himself, panicking, getting depressed and catching the express train to negative town. But it's not easy: I can't tell you how many times I was in the same situation as Tom, panicked and tried to recover to first place by the first mark only to fall even further behind, which seemed only to prove to myself that I was not good in these conditions or the boat was slow or I was a poor thinker.

Engage your logic

One of the keys to resilience is to be able to think strategically and logically. This is a trained skill. Many years ago, for one reason or another, I found myself leaving home in a hurry. I could only take one bag. I was emotional, anxious and down. I went to the city and spent some time wandering around, using payphones to try calling some friends to no avail. It was getting later and later, and I was on Flinders Street in Melbourne with nowhere to go. By this time I had calmed down, and decided I needed a plan. Not one for a night, but a 12-month plan. I sketched it out. One option was to spend the night on the street. The other option was to go home – but with an escape plan. I decided to return home, pass my final uni exams, win the highest-paying position I could and then move out independently to where I wanted to live. After receiving my exam results and getting through the roller-coaster of job interviews, I was offered three positions in one day. (I still remember that day: I literally sat down and cried.) It was my ticket to freedom. Three months after starting my new job, I was settled in my apartment in South Yarra. I often walk past that spot where I made my plan all those years ago, and I never forget that moment when I demonstrated my resilience. (I am also happy to say that my sons, who are older than I was at that time, show no signs of moving out of home!)

Life has provided me with many more moments to demonstrate my resilience. While I was out training for a cycling event on the Sunshine Coast in Queensland a car turned in front of me with no room for me to brake. I slammed into the car and did a lot of damage, including breaking my right hand. It was a devastating blow: I knew I could not race the next day, and that my work as a speaker and workshop facilitator was going to be severely affected. I also knew I would not be back on a bike for some time.

I quickly developed a very fixed, negative mindset about my situation. I was dwelling on the things I couldn't do, particularly when the doctor said I couldn't even train indoors as an elevated heart rate would affect my recovery. But then, luckily, my growth mindset kicked in. I started to think, 'How bad can this be?'. I remembered racing against fellow Knights of Suburbia rider Paul Tindal, who cycles with one arm very successfully. After some more research, I realised that if I could find a bike that had its front brake on the left side of the handlebar I could ride slowly around my local neighbourhood without using my right hand at all, since the front brake does most of the work. More research showed that US and European bikes come standard with the front brake on the left and rear brake on the right, the opposite of Australian bikes. But where could I find a bike like this?

As I sat in my house contemplating this challenge, I looked at my beautiful Somec Time Trial bike that I had secured from the actor Robin Williams' estate after his tragic passing. Robin was a passionate and very fast cyclist who had built up a wonderful collection. It was like a message from Robin himself: get the bike out of the house and ride it. And I did! Just a few slow laps around the neighbourhood, but it was so refreshing and got me motivated to stick to my recovery plan.

Meet Nathanael 'Never Give Up' Zurbrügg

I met Nathanael Zurbrügg through the John Maxwell Team leadership program. My little accident above is like a scratch on a fingernail compared to what Nathanael has been through.

Nathanael was just a year old when he lost his kidneys and was diagnosed with an incurable chronic illness. About three years later, his parents learned that if their son survived, he would never be able to go to school, walk, talk or function independently. Nathanael became hearing impaired when he was four years old. (He says this helps him to only hear what he wants to hear.) Between the ages of five and 11, he experienced three failed kidney transplants.

There is no life without kidneys. To keep him alive, Nathanael has had dialysis treatments three times a week for 4.5 hours each time, over his lifetime. In case you're counting, that's more than 150 free lessons to learn about being persistent, every year.

Even though it was predicted that his life would be hopeless, Nathanael achieved something that he thought would be impossible with his broken body: on the day he turned 30, he ran 30km!

Nathanael says that instead of focusing on what the medical report said about him – what he couldn't do or couldn't have – he made a choice to focus on what God said about him, and what he could still do or still have. He believes our wish to live life to the fullest doesn't need to be defined by limitations; it's defined by what you believe about your potential.

That, my friends, is resilience.

Surround yourself with resilient people

At the J24 World Championships in sailing my team was tested beyond anything we had practised for. On the last leg of the last race on the last day, we were sitting in a solid second place when the old boom (which supports the sail and is second only to the mast in importance on a yacht) snapped in half. My negative voice (Dick) immediately piped up, saying 'Well, there it goes – so close to winning a world championship but denied'. But then I realised our resilient crew were not going to let a little thing like the boom breaking deny us what was rightly ours. So, while Moose (our trusted Mr Fix It) strapped our spinnaker pole to the boom as a brace, which also meant putting holes in our sail to tie the rope to, the rest of us had to hike our lives out to compensate for his 85 kilograms not being out holding the boat flat. We improvised, we got creative (within the rules, of course) and we sailed the downwind leg of our lives. Not only did we retain our second place in the race, but we actually extended our lead on our competitor in third place and closed the gap between us and the leader of the race. This effort gave us the result to seal the world championship.

The lesson here is: when the boom broke my mindset was not as resilient as it needed to be. However, by being surrounded by a team grounded in resilience through years at the top levels of competition, I was able to snap out of my negative mindset. It was an emotional and unforgettable experience in resilience and creativity in sport.

THE IMPORTANCE OF GRATITUDE

'Anyone who gets the opportunity to do what
they love to do and then actually get paid to do it,
you don't take that for granted.'

Jon Bon Jovi

Being grateful, even when life seems to be against you, can be a very helpful perspective. In situations where someone has hurt me or treated me with disrespect, I try to ask myself: 'What did this teach me? What is there to be grateful for in this situation?'

Some people advise you should carry a gratitude diary, and write down all the things you are grateful for each day. I like to use the notes app on my phone, so I can refer back to my list easily. If I am writing the name of a person on my list – someone who has helped me in some way, or gone out of their way to assist – I always ask myself: 'have I reached out and thanked them?'. My friend Sue Barrett, author of *142 Days of Gratitude That Changed My Life Forever* says that, 'The practice of gratitude moves us away from myopic thinking. It helps us to uncover connections, find pathways and reveal relationships. Gratitude extends our frame of reference from a cropped narcissistic selfie to a panoramic tapestry of life in its fullest glory.'

You need to be intentional about gratitude, otherwise it is very easy to let the stresses of life carry you away and you forget all the things you have to be thankful for.

Henry Winkler, who played 'The Fonz' in the classic sitcom *Happy Days* (and now seems to be cast in almost every Adam Sandler movie), was once asked by a BBC journalist about the secret to his longevity in the entertainment industry. He said, 'Tenacity and gratitude – and thank you for allowing me to come on and talk about my work'. So, be tenacious and be grateful – it's all possible for you.

Be a one-minute possibility person

It only takes one minute to:

- Ask someone how they feel today
- Inspire someone
- Make someone laugh
- Thank someone
- Connect with someone on social media
- Like someone's post on social media
- Tell someone they are needed
- Tell someone they are loved
- Set a higher goal
- Commit to change
- Drink more water
- Eat some fruit or veg
- Smile
- Face a fear
- Be quiet
- Get changed into exercise clothes.

4. Step 2: Building your vision

'Your vision is like driving your car at night to a destination 100km away. You know where you are going but your headlights will only show you the next 300m, not the next 100km. The path you take will reveal itself along the way.'

John C Maxwell

Vision, dream, goal, purpose ... many people get hung up here and lose their momentum – don't be one of them. My 4-Step Possibility System© works perfectly whether you are chasing a dream or goal, or pursuing your vision or purpose. I know each of these has its own definition but don't get hung up on which one works for you. Whether it's a goal, a vision, a dream or a purpose, it all comes down to the 'why' that is driving you at this point in your life.

As you mature in life, you will probably find your vision and purpose will evolve and become clearer as you develop as a person and experience life. That said, you do need to be very clear about what your vision, dream or goal is if you truly want to achieve what is possible for you. The clearer your 'why' is, the easier it will be to visualise yourself accomplishing it, and for others to understand it and support you in the process.

What I don't want you to do is have paralysis by analysis as you search for your unique purpose in life. I have seen people get sidetracked, become listless and even have mild depression because they haven't nailed down their vision. I tend to find this a very Western world issue. When I travel to Asia, for example,

I find everyone so busy living and working they don't have much time to contemplate their future.

However, success leaves clues, and one of the ways to discover your purpose is to listen to yourself. This is how I have approached life, and while it has led me to change careers four times while always having a side hustle on the go, I wouldn't have it any other way. I have worked with many people in a multitude of roles in my time, and all these experiences have been worthwhile.

SCRATCH THE ITCH

When I was growing up, my father wanted me to study medicine because it would lead to a well-paid career. There were two problems with that: firstly, I didn't like medicine; and secondly, I was not smart enough to get anywhere near the marks I needed. Trust me: if you are pursuing medicine you need to have a passion for it, whether you're aspiring to be a surgeon, GP or nurse. They are amazing people.

Accounting was the next best thing for me. Business I loved, but accounting? Not so much. I got high distinctions in all my marketing and business development subjects at uni, and credits in subjects involving debits and credits. As I said, success leaves clues. But I was determined and passionate, and ended up working in accounting roles at KPMG, Rio Tinto and Kraft Foods (Kraft Heinz).

But I had an itch. That itch was an entrepreneurial one. I was brought up in small business, raced yachts with entrepreneurs and business owners and could not work for only a salary year in, year out. I liked the concept of risk and reward for effort. Later on, I realised I was actually an 'intrapreneur'. When I was asked to join a small computer dealer at the start of the personal computer revolution I said yes, trading my taxation accountant role for the wild west of the personal computer business. My mentor was astounded, my boss bewildered and my parents lost for words. Luckily my girlfriend, later to be my wife, was supportive – as she always is.

It turned out to be a great move. Within a year, I was recruited by Apple's largest Australian corporate reseller and won (with the help of an amazing team) the largest ever corporate deal for Apple in Australia at that time. Incidentally, my two biggest clients were KPMG and Rio Tinto. Life is truly about swings and round-abouts; as they say, never blow a relationship – you never know when it will come back around. After that, I went to work for Apple itself – the greatest toy shop in the world, we used to call it.

Recently I was in Los Angeles with my middle son Finn – a filmmaker who is studying screenwriting. We were at the Warner Brothers Lot being treated to the most amazing guided tour. The guide was incredible. He knew everybody and was constantly darting off the regular tour and, on his radio, working out how to give us the best possible experience. We managed to go on the sets of *The Ellen Show*, *Friends* and more. After the tour, I asked him about his passion. He told me he was a film and TV industry fanatic from Miami who attended a tour at Warner Brothers just like we had done. After the tour he knew he had to be involved in filmmaking. So, he left his home and family in Miami and moved to Los Angeles. He had secured a part-time job at Warner Brothers and was studying film. I asked him what made him leave his family and move across America. He replied, 'You just have to scratch that itch'.

My friend Sarah Blanck had just returned from finishing fourth overall in sailing at the Olympics (sailing a yacht that she was unfamiliar with, I might add) when she decided to start a new career as a graphic designer. But as she sat working, she found her gaze drifting out the window as she observed the weather, wondering what the wind was doing and which direction it was coming from. After a while, she realised that her interest in the weather was due to the fact that she wasn't 'done' with the Olympics: she wanted to give it another go. And that's exactly what she did.

Remember, though, that even if you discover a new purpose or vision for a better life, it doesn't mean you should drop everything and pursue it. The world is patient, and so should you be. Plus, there are ways you can move towards your vision without turning your world upside down. For example: if you want to explore your creative side, you could practice it part-time, start a new course at uni, build your first website or attend an inspirational event.

My wife, Leisa, is my business partner. She is also a photographer and artist, and was a teacher when we met. I was in IT at the time, but that didn't stop us from starting a photography business as a side hustle. We had a lot of fun photographing the Melbourne music scene in the 1990s, with Leisa behind the camera and me writing the articles for the industry newspapers. I found it made life a lot easier for the editors of these publications if we could provide both the photos and the story for them. It was an early lesson in sales and PR that would help me many times in my life.

Sometimes it's the right goal but the wrong timing, and that's okay

Sometimes all the stars seem to align and you set off to pursue your dream – but then, it doesn't work out.

This happened to me after a large global project I was involved with was disbanded, and the entire team retrenched. I believed it was the right time to branch out on my own. It wasn't.

The whole experience changed my approach to work. While I went back to 'working for the man', I changed careers to get more experience in my weaker areas. I saw my next couple of full-time roles as steps to a higher goal – not as my final destination. It all worked out in the end – and I was well prepared to take the leap to self-employment when the right time presented itself.

Don't be dismayed if it takes a little longer, and a few more steps than expected, before you achieve your vision.

WRITE IT OUT

Once you have settled on a vision or purpose, it is vital to write it out with as much clarity as possible. Be as specific as you can, but also remember brevity is better than meaningless, repetitive words – especially if you are planning to share your vision with others because you will need them to buy into it and not be confused by it.

Now, you may be tempted to avoid putting your vision down on paper because you view it as your personal vision, not to be shared. Fair point, but I challenge you to move past this. Here is why: no person is an island. I have never met a truly self-made person; everyone has a team working for them, with them or alongside them. As soon as you decide on a dream, a vision or a goal, the next step is to select your 'Dream Team' to help you bring it to fruition.

Test it with your team

When I am running goal-setting and change-management workshops with organisations I get them to focus on the acronym UCOP. This stands for:

U   Does your team **understand** it?

C   Did they get a chance to **contribute** to it?

O   Do they feel they **own** it with you?

P   Do they have the passion and understanding to
      pass it onto others?

The contribution part is a vital step for any team. In the brilliant
book *The Leadership Challenge*, Professors Kouzes and Posner
identify a key practice of a world-class leader: the ability to
inspire a shared vision. This means that, if you are a leader (and
let's face it, if you are a parent you are also a leader), you don't
need the vision to be 100 per cent complete before you share it.
It's best to have your team contribute to it as well, so they feel a
sense of ownership – this will mean the vision is reached far more
quickly and easily.

In chapter 2 I told you about the vision my wife and I created
when we decided to move house. What I didn't mention is that
we shared this vision with our boys, who added some great ideas
and thoughts we had not considered. This gave them buy-in, and
helped them to feel like achieving the vision was a team effort
with rewards for everyone. So, when we had to spend that time
looking for houses, measuring and researching and, eventually,
those long days packing and unpacking (does anyone actually
enjoy that part?) it was a lot easier to get their cooperation and
assistance. It's no different in business.

Now what?

Some people say that once your vision is written, you should file
it away and let the law of attraction bring it to you as you focus
on the strategies and actions to achieve it. Others will tell you it's
better to keep the vision alive and visible on your phone, on your
desk, in the bathroom – wherever you will see it every day to
reinforce it. I have used both techniques and both work for me.

The main point is that you need to be able to imagine the
vision already realised – not only being able to see, but also

feel what it will be like when it is achieved. My mentor Paul Martinelli has as his email sign off: 'Hold your image'. You could extend this to: 'Hold your image and feeling'. The point is, it is vital to put this vision and feeling in the present tense as if you have already achieved it. This will motivate you to see it through.

Let's say your vision is to bring joy to people through mentoring youth. What does that look like? How will you feel having achieved this vision? When you do this, you are setting a vision with intentionality. That is a very powerful force.

Don't let your vision of the future remain blurry because of the constraints of the present.

I am the greatest

One of the most high-profile pioneers of vision in action (although many misinterpreted him as a loudmouth) was 'The Greatest' Muhammad Ali.

I would recommend listening to his words and language. While he was a great marketer and a PR dream when he spoke, he was also very intentional. He would say 'I am' and 'I do' rather than 'I will be' or 'I plan to'. He always spoke of his dreams in the present tense, like he had already achieved them – because in his mind, he had.

VISUALISATION

You can practise this with your staff, or your children if you are a parent. One of the powerful side effects of visualisation is that the mind can play out your desired future state in incredible detail, and it will trigger the muscles in your body even though you are not actually doing the activity. The concept is the same as if you were using a virtual reality device – but this version is free, and always available!

My eldest son Ben would use visualisation before racing his motocross bike as a 10-year-old. He would lie in bed the night before a race and visualise the perfect lap. What was interesting about this was that his mind would create alerts to ensure he did get the perfect lap. Many times I would think he was asleep when he would yell out: 'Dad, did you check the rear tyre pressure?'. He knew that to get the perfect start and the right approach to the first corner, his rear tyre had better be correctly inflated.

When I won the 1994 J24 World Sailing Championship with US sailing legend Ken Read I used visualisation a lot. I knew I had to start thinking on a much higher level: Ken was already a six-times world champion, business leader and sailing professional. I needed to feel like I was on his level to work as a team with him. Also, the crew I was to sail with were all professionals in the sailing and marine industry. Racing yachts was something they did as a career, whereas at that in point in my life, marketing IT systems was my main gig. I knew we would have no time to race together prior to the first race, either, so it was vital I was at least in the team from a mindset point of view. The key I learned here was to focus on the end goal: winning the world championship. I focused my visualisation on being awarded the trophy for first place over and over and over, and then my subconscious worked backwards through the conscious mind to ensure the right steps were taken to give my vision the best possible chance of coming true.

But what happens when it doesn't go well – when in real life we make a mistake? I recall an interview with golfer Tiger Woods when he explained his approach to this issue. He said that, after the game, he would always recall the mistakes and errors he made. Then he would visualise himself perfecting the previous poor shot. Once perfected in his mind, he would let it go – he wouldn't dwell on the error, or even think of it again. It was his way of erasing the subconscious mind's memory of the poor shot, and replacing it with a powerful visual of him succeeding.

Example vision statements

Now, your vision statement might be entirely different to the ones I have listed below – and that's okay! But maybe these will give you some inspiration:

- **TED:** 'To spread ideas.'
- **Starbucks:** 'To inspire and nurture the human spirit – one person, one cup and one neighbourhood at a time.'
- **Amazon:** 'To be Earth's most customer-centric company.'
- **Australian Government Department of Health:** 'Better health and wellbeing for all Australians, now and for future generations.'
- **Oxfam:** 'A just world without poverty.'
- **Nike:** 'To bring inspiration and innovation to every athlete* in the world. (*If you have a body, you are an athlete.)'
- **RSPCA:** 'To prevent cruelty to animals by actively promoting their care and protection.'
- **Rob Hartnett 1994:** 'To be a world-class sailor.'
- **Rob Hartnett 2019:** 'To inspire and equip people to be Possibility Seekers and Leaders.'

YOUR DREAM DOES NOT NEED TO DIE OF OLD AGE

Peter Mounsey, a 91-year-old man from Adelaide, broke speed records when he took his classic 1940s Velocette motorcycle (without rear suspension) to a speed of 93.8mph. Peter had a strong vision (he wanted to exceed 91mph on his Velocette), backed up with a team to assist and coach, repetitive attempts and a thirst for learning and continual growth. He is now aiming to exceed 100mph in 2020!

Robert Marchand from France held the one-hour distance record for cycling at 14 miles in an hour. You might not think that is much, except that the category was for 100 to 105-year-olds! He is 107 years old in 2019 and celebrated his birthday with a solid group ride with his young friends. He also only started cycling and exercising when he retired from work.

These days, while I am older and wiser, my cycling, coaching program and eating habits have brought me back to the weight I was 30 years ago. I am aerobically fitter than I have ever been.

33 years trying for a Cube .

Like all Laser sailors globally, I had always coveted a Laser Cube – a trophy unique to the Laser that was only awarded based on entries. I had sailed the Laser class for some 30 years and gone close a number of times to winning a Cube, but I was never successful. In fact, my eldest son Ben won his first Cube as a sixteen-year-old, and in his first major Laser regatta. So, while we had one in the family, I didn't have my own!

At a Laser Masters regatta, there was an opportunity for a small group of sailors to be personally coached by the Olympic Gold Medallist and World Champion Tom Burton. I had known Tom for a few years and he had always been approachable and down to earth. I first thought Tom would be great and then my little voice Richard, being a Dick, said: 'What if he thinks you suck, what if he says after the first race, 'Look, Rob, I don't think you are coachable''. But the opportunity was too good to pass up. I called Dick a Dick and signed up.

Despite my fears, I sailed well in the first race of the day and it was a highlight to this day to get a top-ten result and sail over to Tom and ask his advice for the next race. Tom was a great coach, he called things as he saw them and wasn't shy to point out any rookie errors. Cruel but fair with a smile was how Tom coached, showing us Masters why he won the Olympic Gold Medal in Rio. Was it worth it signing up with Tom, doing extra coaching sessions and briefings post-race when all I wanted was to rest? Absolutely! As he helped me achieve second overall in my age group, and I secured my first-ever Laser Cube after 33 years in the class. Never give up on the dream!

MAKE TIME FOR MARGIN

Every high-performance car, motorcycle, bicycle, go-kart, yacht and windsurfer is pulled down, repaired and rejuvenated between racing events. No-one would expect Lewis Hamilton to drive the same car week in, week out without maintenance, servicing and renewal. It is no different when it comes to you.

If you want to be a high performer you must, as part of your systems and processes, schedule renewal time for your mind and your body. Too many entrepreneurs and intrapreneurs run themselves into the ground. It's not healthy, and it's not productive. If you do push yourself to the limit continuously your body will react, and it will actually shut you down for rest before too long. This is what happens when you get the flu, colds, glandular fever and other illnesses. Your immune system becomes depleted, and the body needs time to build its strength back up.

Margin also helps in the process of deciding on your vision. Unless you give yourself space to think, to breathe and to slow down, your vision will be very limited and you'll be at risk of pursuing something you are good at, but don't actually enjoy. Margin gives you the space you need to really consider what you want from life.

One of the strategies I have implemented is one I learned from an entrepreneur, who said: 'I can get 12 months' work done in

10 months but I can't get 12 months' done in 12'. The point is, if you want to have a highly productive year you need to allocate a good portion to planning, rest, rejuvenation and thinking. This is called creating margin in your life. Margin is the difference between what you are capable of if you push yourself to the limit every single day, and what you are doing. If they are same thing then you have a problem.

	What I am capable of doing
NO MARGIN	What I am currently doing

	What I am capable of doing
MARGIN	
	What I am currently doing

This margin in your life is for creative, big-picture thinking. Mark Cole, CEO of the John Maxwell Company, explained that he actually made an error when creating what he thought was margin. Mark was regularly scheduling time for himself (which was a great start), but what he was using the margin time for was to solve all the issues, problems and challenges that he had already come across. In other words, he was not creating margin to rebuild, think, create and innovate but instead to solving already existing issues.

Margin is different. If you are a leader and you want your team to be more productive you must create margin for them. Not just by telling them it is a good idea, but by actually scheduling it in on a weekly or monthly basis for them.

Chief economist Joe Davis of Vanguard, a funds provider that manages some $5.4 trillion of wealth, told me that he expects his people to be innovative, creative and to test theories and ideas that might impact the future. Not only does he ask this of his team, but he allocates a percentage of their work time each week to creative time and he checks in to see what creative new areas they are working on that will enhance their thinking. This is a great example of leader-led margin.

Consider margin when you are coming up with your vision. You might even want to incorporate some words about margin or how you will keep your brain healthy and creative when you are writing down your vision.

BURNOUT

Many people suffer from burnout. It is unfortunate, and it can lead to major health issues if it is a regular occurrence. Burnout sometimes feels like you have hit a wall. You lack motivation, you lack energy and often you will simply shut down. This is your body saying: 'I need rest, and if you are not going to give it to me I will take charge of things myself'. This happened to me when I contracted glandular fever. It literally knocked me out for three weeks and it stayed with me on and off for 10 years. Even now I can sense its symptoms when I need to slow down.

So, what does burnout have to do with your vision? I believe if you are clear about and focused on your primary vision (rather than the millions of smaller goals you are probably trying to work towards right now) you are less likely to face burnout. I also recommend incorporating wellness and stress management into your vision if this is something that you have struggled with in the past.

A strategy I have found to avoid burnout is the Eisenhower Matrix, developed by Dwight D Eisenhower – the 34th President of the United States. If you combine the Eisenhower Matrix with a strategy of delegating to others it will have the effect of skilling and empowering your team, as well as freeing you up to focus on the top left quadrant – the important and urgent tasks.

	URGENT	NOT URGENT
IMPORTANT	**DO NOW** Due soon Aligned to goals Leverages my skills/role	**SCHEDULE IN CALENDAR** Due later Aligned to goals Leverages my skills/role
NOT IMPORTANT	**DELEGATE AUTOMATE DECLINE** Due soon Not aligned to goals Someone else could do it	**DECLINE DELEGATE** Due later Not aligned to goals Someone else could do it

The most inspiring example of a world-class leader who prioritises margin in his life is Jack Dorsey. Jack is the CEO and founder of Twitter and Square, and you can follow him on Twitter (duh!) @ jackdorsey. Jack does not carry a laptop (he works mostly from his iPhone and uses the 'notes' app to great effect). He walks to and from work listening to podcasts. He also meditates regularly.

MEDITATION AND MINDFULNESS

Margin can take other forms as well. One of the ways I have found most productive for spending margin time is meditation, and I have found the practice of meditation helps me to create visions and goals that are aligned with what I really want out of life.

I had always been fascinated by meditation but could not make it stick or get what I wanted from books and audio programs. That was until I decided to seek out professional guidance. The first person who really helped me understand its power and how to do it properly was Roger Hart. Some of you might know Roger as the lead singer and guitarist from the '80s band 'Little Heroes'. Roger packed in the rock star life after becoming despondent with the music industry and set off to find a bigger meaning to life. During this time he studied all manner of religions and techniques and wrote a wonderful book called *Happy to Burn*, which is all about how to use the power of meditation in today's busy, time-poor world. It was the first book that showed me that meditation was a mindset, and you did not necessarily need to sit cross-legged in a robe to enjoy its benefits. Roger was also kind enough to meet with me and answer my questions when he visited Melbourne.

Following Roger's insistence that there was something worth pursuing in meditation, I continued my growth mindset approach and soon discovered Transcendental Meditation (TM) in a great book by Bob Roth. Bob's book, which follows the work of Maharishi Mahesh Yogi (spiritual adviser to the Beatles!) was truly a revelation. The Maharishi was actually a scientist, who proved that meditation provided untold health benefits. Bob Roth, a lawyer (and they don't come more sceptical than lawyers), reluctantly tried meditation. He was soon convinced, and studied under the Maharishi for many years.

'I use my memory but I do not let my memory use me.'

Maharishi Mahesh Yogi

TM is incredibly simple to do once you have mastered it. But what I learned from Roger and Bob is that TM must be approached seriously and with intent. You must be intentional about creating margin to enable your spiritual growth. Ideally, you would do a course taught by a trained professional so that you really understand the principles. This is where I went wrong at first: I had been reading about meditation but not really understanding it, as I had not been applying it properly with a coach – I lacked the skill. After I committed to a course, I realised that there was way more to it than I imagined – but it is so worthwhile. I am still in my early days of TM, but there are many exceptional practitioners who were taught by Bob Roth and swear by its power. A few you will have heard of are David Lynch, Jerry Seinfeld, Ellen DeGeneres, Kristen Bell, Martina Navratilova, Russell Brand, Clint Eastwood (who has practised TM for over 40 years) and Ray Dalio.

Jerry Seinfeld credits TM with helping him get through nine years of *Seinfeld*. When the crew would take a break for lunch, Jerry would take himself off for 30 minutes of TM. Ray Dalio says that when he knows he has a big day of meetings, he meditates using TM for at least two hours.

SETTLING ON YOUR VISION

By now, hopefully you have a vision written down and you have come up with a strategy for keeping your vision top of mind. Let's now do a little test to check you are happy with it.
Ask yourself:

- If this vision were possible, what would it look like?

- What would my vision require of me?

- What does my heart think of it?

- What parts of it are clear?
- What parts are still unclear?
- Does my vision move me?

Now it's time to implement your vision by designing a strategy to achieve it.

5. Step 3: Developing your strategy

'Nothing is impossible,
it just means it hasn't been done yet.'

Travis Pastrana

The 'strategy' part of my 4-Step Possibility System© is where we start to develop the 'how' to achieve our 'why'. This is where we start to identify the building blocks that we'll need to put in place for our vision to come to fruition.

First, let's look at some example strategies based on the visions we saw in the previous chapter.

	Vision	**Strategy**
Starbucks	'To inspire and nurture the human spirit – one person, one cup and one neighbourhood at a time.'	1. Own all the stores and drive the brand message 2. Have consistent, high-quality customer service 3. Open up in neighborhoods across the world
Amazon	'To be Earth's most customer-centric company.'	1. Launch world's largest online bookstore 2. Launch world's largest online marketplace

	Vision	**Strategy**
Rob Hartnett 1994	'To be a world-class sailor.'	1. Win a world sailing championship within 12 months 2. Compete in two world championships 3. Compete in a variety of different style boats 4. Increase fitness and decrease body fat

A key point that you will hopefully have observed in these examples is that even when the vision is solid, our strategies might not work (or they might only partially work). Amazon made some expensive mistakes trying to get its auction strategy to work, and it wasn't until it changed tactics to develop Amazon Marketplace that its original idea from 1999 become a profitable reality. Starbucks expanded too quickly and attempted to break into the wrong markets (e.g. Melbourne, which already had a thriving coffee culture focused on quality local cafés) and had to reassess its strategy – but the vision remained the same.

My dream was to become a world-class sailor. My strategy was to do two world championships in a year. I did win the first world championship so decided not to do the second one. This was a decision I made as circumstances changed. This illustrates the importance of being a bit flexible with your strategy. Be emotional and passionate about your vision, but keep the emotions out of how you are going to achieve it.

LITTLE BIG THINGS

Little Big Things are the four or five key areas that will make the biggest difference to achieving your dream. It's a good idea to pinpoint these, otherwise you can easily confuse activity with achievement (and they are very different things). Do you know anybody who always seems to be busy and multitasking but they don't seem to make much progress year-on-year? They probably don't know about Little Big Things!

When I was aiming to win the world sailing championships my Little Big Things were:

- Right boat
- Right crew
- Right equipment
- Right location
- Rules and regulations.

To show you how flexible this is, let me apply it to the road cycling World Masters Games I competed in; my Little Big Things were:

- Right bike
- Right fitness
- Right equipment
- Right location
- Rules and regulations.

Let me now apply it to starting an entrepreneurial business to show you how it's usually just four to five Little Big Things that make the difference:

- Right business structure
- Right fit for your goals

- Right sales, marketing and service
- Right product or services
- Right finance and accounting systems.

FINDING THE RIGHT FIT

When you're developing your strategy, it helps to have a good understanding of your own personality and work preferences so you can devise a plan that is the right fit for both your goals and your preferred way of working.

From what you read in the press about entrepreneurship, it seems that every successful business owner is a millennial dressed like a hipster with a start-up that has made a billion dollars. The reality is that anyone can be a successful entrepreneur or businessperson – no matter your age or stage of life, or whether you have goals to pursue your own business or achieve success in your corporate job. You just need to work out the type of business mindset you have, and work with your own strengths.

Business owners tend to fall into three categories:[7]

- **Empire builders:** they want to go big: big businesses, big portfolios, big risks. They like to negotiate and make deals, they are extremely competitive and they are happy to aggressively leverage, take on joint ventures and borrow money.

- **Lifestyle builders:** they crave freedom and choice, and work to live (not live to work). They prefer to 'set and forget' so they have time to live the life they want.

- **Intrapreneurs:** the company rebels! They want autonomy and creativity, but not the risk. They like to lead, but don't have to have the huge corner office. If they do have their own business it is probably a side hustle, or a franchise – to suit their lower risk threshold.

None of the above are more right or wrong than each other, but liberate yourself and remove all the friction by deciding/accepting which one you are. Then allow yourself to behave accordingly, stop comparing yourself to the other types (after all, they all have their downsides) and create your plan that fits your profile.

Remember that we can also move between these entrepreneurial mindsets. I know many people who have started as intrapreneurs and decided the corporate life was not for them (or got fired for being too creative or disruptive!) and become lifestyle investors or empire builders. Others have started as empire builders and then become lifestyle investors as age and finances allowed for a different set of motivations. Many entrepreneurs go back to full-time roles as intrapreneurs for a time due to financial or family reasons. But you need to decide at this point what feels most right for you, and then pursue your strategy based on this decision.

YOUR DREAM DELIVERY TEAM

Once you start to plan your strategy, you may begin to see gaps in your expertise, skills, ability, financial or geographical location to accomplish the vision. Whenever you see a limitation, you will need to either skill up or hire up depending upon your timing, availability of finance and inclination for studying and practicing the skill you are missing.

If you know anything about cycling, you will probably recognise the name Peter Sagan. While he has not won a Tour de France, he has won the sprint category several times and he is a three-times world champion. In his book *My World*, Peter talks a lot about 'Team Peter'. Team Peter includes Peter's cycling champion brother Yuraj, and a wider team of mechanics, managers, masseurs, coaches and support staff. When Peter changed cycling teams, Team Peter went along with him. As you can see, while cycling may appear to be a single-person sport, it really isn't.

I used this example of Team Peter in one of my leadership workshops, and before the end of the day one of the participants had started to sketch out 'Team Ashley'. He had several vacant slots in his team, which I really liked – he knew he needed expertise in these areas, but was unsure as yet who he would turn to. What a great approach to intentional growth. So, I encourage you all to think about who is in your Team Rob, Team Fiona, Team Abdhul, Team Christina.

Your team also plays a big part in your resilience. When you experience a knock down or knock back it can be very easy to spiral in a negative direction. If you have a good, trusted team, you can rely on them to support you by listening and perhaps reframing the issue in a different way. Remember: we see the world not as it is, but as we think it is.

MAKE PEOPLE PART OF YOUR STRATEGY

I have to admit that I am not a networker. I dislike the word, and whenever I receive an event invitation that says 'plenty of time for networking' I am the first one to say 'sorry, not available'.

However, I can also tell you that my network has been the key to my success in both the corporate world and my current career as a business owner. Not once has a job ad led me to a new position – I have almost always found new roles through my personal connections. When I was ready to strike out on my own (the second time), it was my network that allowed me to start my own business profitably without having to borrow funds. I'm also certain that the power of your personal network is even more important today than it was for me in the early stages of my career – the internet and social media can do amazing things for you, but only if you embrace the possibilities.

Networking needs to be intentional. By that, I mean you and the other person both need to bring something valuable to the connection, and be clear about what you hope to gain.

If you're just starting out in networking, here are my tips for getting it right:

- Choose who to approach with intention. Be clear about exactly what type of role or opportunity you want, and think about who you might approach who might be able to assist.

- Have credibility. Be open and sincere.

- Ask for guidance and advice – not a job.

- Be realistic about what you are asking for.

- Demonstrate that you are serious about the opportunity and have put in the effort to research it.

- Think about how you can bring value to the other person, either now or in the future. What goes around comes around.

In the early 2000s I was looking to make a move to a large global advertising agency as I had enjoyed working with creative teams in my days at HP. I sought guidance from some contacts at the larger agencies, who suggested I join a small firm and 'do my apprenticeship' – working for a small business means you get to experience many roles simply because the employees need to wear multiple hats. I did this for several years and learned so much. When it came time to step up from the small marketing agency to a global advertising firm, I knew I would need to engage my network again to find someone who could give me the inside scoop on what was going on in global advertising – but because I now had experience, I could be more specific about the role I wanted which was in digital and direct marketing.

A few years earlier I had purchased my first Porsche from the managing director of a global ad agency, who also happened to be a sailor. We had kept in touch over the years, so I reconnected with him and asked if he would meet me for a coffee. My intention was not to ask him for a job, but to seek his guidance and advice.

This took a call and some meetings. He wanted to know how serious I was, what I had done, who I knew and how committed I was to this direction. He gave me some great strategies, and a few months later called saying he had an opportunity that might suit. We caught up again and he made some introductions, and after about two months of meetings I received an offer from a connection he introduced me to.

The role I took on was 'off market', so it was never advertised. This happens more than you'd think – it saves the employer recruitment costs, and onboarding is typically faster with results coming quicker because the new employee is already familiar with the employer and ready to make things happen (this was certainly the case with me).

Why did my contact assist me? Well, not only did he get to help me into an industry he was passionate about, he also helped another of his colleagues out by helping him fill the vacant role. It also provided him with two happy connections he could work with in the future.

When I eventually left that role to start my own business, this contact was one of the people I called on to assist me as a commercial partner on several projects. What goes around, comes around.

DEVELOPING A STRATEGY TO LEAD YOUR TEAM

Leadership does not necessarily mean you are a CEO or leading hundreds of people. If you are a parent or guardian, you are a leader. If you run a small business, you are probably a leader. I don't believe in 'born leaders': leadership is a learned skill, just like any other. Steve Jobs was a very different leader when he came back to Apple the second time around, according to his longtime work colleague, friend and the man they call the 'Trillion Dollar Coach', Bill Campbell.

I have been fortunate to work with, sail with and be guided by many great leaders. They are not household names, but that's the point: leaders don't need to be famous to be effective. Here are my criteria for great leaders, inspired in part by James Kouzes and Barry Posner.[8]

Great leaders go first

The best leaders lead by example. They know the behaviour they expect, and they demonstrate it themselves. John C Maxwell says it well: 'A leader knows the way, goes the way and shows the way'. So many people in leadership positions today essentially say: 'Do as I say, not as I do'. My advice is to avoid doing this: everyone sees through it and nobody will follow you for long. Being an effective leader takes effort. I know this sounds obvious, but you would be surprised how many leaders assume their people understand them and their direction when they send out an email or rely on their corporate communications team to transmit the message. I have been lucky to serve under some wonderful leaders like the late Lew Platt, CEO and President of Hewlett-Packard (HP). Lew used to do a quarterly call to all 145 000 employees, and then backed this up with slide deck. He also travelled extensively to connect in person to his global team. If Lew could do it, so can any other leader – and he did not even have the luxury of tools such as Skype, Salesforce Chatter or Cloud Video.

Great leaders inspire

This is what I see missing in so many leaders: they are simply not inspiring. Either they are not inspired themselves or they don't have the communication skills to inspire others – or, sometimes, both. Think about the great leaders in your life. Were any of them uninspiring? I bet not. The best leaders I have worked with have all been inspiring and motivating.

Great leaders are connectors, not climbers

The best leader understands that his or her role is to create more leaders. Poor leaders work to ensure only they are seen as a leader, and will do anything to protect their position. Great leaders connect to other leaders frequently and are always looking to the next challenge, asking themselves which capabilities they will need in their leaders into the future.

Great leaders encourage a shared vision

As we discussed in chapter 4, great leaders don't come up with a vision and say, 'It's my way or the highway'. Great leaders want to create a shared vision that their team, direct reports or virtual workers co-create. Great leaders use the acronym UCOP, which we worked through in chapter 4, when they want to create a shared vision that will be successful.

Great leaders appoint influencers as first followers

To be a leader of scale you need to have good people who are influencers and can create their own loyalty and following. As a leader, it is easy to reward the most loyal person – but if they are not respected by others, you will only create an army of two rather than a movement. (Check out my YouTube channel for a great video about this.)

Great leaders challenge people and processes

Great leaders don't accept that the status quo is the best way. They challenge processes and limited thinking, and get their hackles up whenever they hear a phrase like: 'But that's the way we have always done it'. They question whether process equals productivity or the opposite, and they challenge their teams to be proactive in providing feedback when systems and processes are not working for them.

Great leaders reward results

Great leaders measure what matters. They reward those who make the effort to change: be it by adopting a new system or process, making a personal sacrifice, accepting a new way of operating, or simply contributing positively to the new direction.

Leadership in action: *Mad Max*

George Miller and the late Byron Kennedy were living in Sydney in the mid 1970s. George was an emergency ward doctor and Byron was a filmmaker in Melbourne. They had an idea for a futuristic movie based on high-speed motorcycles and motorcars with police versus outlaws and a very sketchy government. The movie they had in mind was *Mad Max*. In 2019 we celebrate the 40th anniversary of the first *Mad Max* movie, which went on to spawn four others, gain a cult following, experience global box office success and catapult George Miller from the emergency ward to fame as one of the world's great directors.

However, what many don't know is that George and Byron employed positive leadership practices in order to make such an iconic movie on the smallest of budgets.

They modelled the way

They used their own hard assets, including their own vans, caravans and cars, in the movie. They were prepared to destroy those things if it meant their vision would become reality. (This meant there were several 'one-take shots' in the film, as they had no budget for a second one!)

They inspired and created a vision

The lead actors – Mel Gibson and Steve Bisley – fully bought in to the vision. In his book *All the Burning Bridges*, Steve Bisley says from the moment he met George he was intrigued. That night, after reading the script, he was determined to play the role of Goose. Clint Eastwood once said that if you get the casting right, 75 per cent of the movie is done. Think about that in your organisation. Have you got the right people in the right roles? Do they believe in your vision? Are they with you?

They were connectors, not climbers

Both George and Byron were both interested in the outcome and understood that without connections they were unlikely to succeed. They wanted to work with actors and filmmakers who believed in their story, not people who had big reputations and would make them look good. The two lead actors were barely out of film school, yet were perfect for the project because they were so passionate.

They enabled and empowered others

They took advice and guidance, and empowered the actors and crew to have a say in how the project rolled out. Hugh Keays-Byrne (the Toecutter) organised the actors in the film, who were to play the roles of his motorcycle gang members, to ride from Sydney to Melbourne so they could bond as a cohesive group.

He also came up with all sorts of ideas and new lines that George and Byron hadn't thought of. He wasn't paid any more for doing that – he just wanted to do the job right. Hugh was the perfect influencer: he was talented, a trained Shakespearian actor, respected by his fellow actors and could ride a motorcycle.

They challenged the process

A movie had never been filmed in this way before *Mad Max*. Lead camera operator David Eggby, a keen motorcyclist, built his own crane for the cameras, put it on his own F100 truck and did some of the most amazing camera work that has ever been seen. His techniques are still used on movies today.

They rewarded effort

Several of the key people who worked for George and Byron, including Mel Gibson and Hugh Keays-Byrne, were rewarded with further involvement in the *Mad Max* series in the years to come.

SITUATIONAL LEADERSHIP

You don't have to be producing a large project such as a movie to demonstrate these key principles. Leadership is situational; you don't need the title of a leader to act as a leader. There are times in life when leadership is needed, and anybody who has the capacity and capability can step up.

I ride with a cycling group called the Knights of Suburbia (KOS). KOS was formed by two ex-footballers turned cyclists David Rigney (Riggo Man) and Russell Lee, who wanted to raise awareness for mental health and suicide prevention. They teamed up with ex-Australian Football League (AFL) player Lance Picioane (whom we met in chapter 1), founder of the charity Love Me Love You.

On a recent ride, I found myself riding above my limit several times as we road into a strong wind. As we reached the two thirds point on the return journey the mind games started: 'Maybe I should stop early. I do have a busy day. I am moving offices today so I really don't have time to be here. There are plenty of other KOS riders who will make it back and represent us well'. (I am sure you have had similar thoughts when pushed to your physical limits.)

Then I got dropped from the lead bunch of 10 riders and just as I was about to pull out I felt a hand on my shoulder. Before I could say anything, he said: 'Let's go get em', champ', and with that he dropped in front of me and I found myself protected from the wind as we rode up towards the leading group. I wondered who the man was, and it was then that I noticed the ink on his spinning legs: It was none other than our fearless leader, Riggo Man.

After the race I was rewarded not only with a much-needed coffee but with some great conversations with many fellow Knights, who had come from all over Melbourne for the event. I was so grateful for Riggo Man's help. It turned out that he had travelled from the other side of the city – further than any of us – to show his support for the ride and to support KOS.

So, let's reflect back on Riggo Man's actions and the leadership practices he demonstrated:

- He modelled the way by finding me and leading me back to the group

- He inspired me by showing up despite it being a great distance from his home and work

- He created an inspired vision and spurred me on to follow him

- He empowered me to find energy I didn't think I had

- I was rewarded with the coffee and camaraderie after the race, among fellow riders who believed in the same cause.

Funnily enough, it was my son Finn who made the most profound observation of Riggo Man that I had missed as I recounted this story to him. Finn, a fine young leader himself, said: 'Dad that's what leaders do: they lead. Riggo Man didn't just go for a ride, he went out to lead others'. That really resonated with me. How many of us wake up in the morning with the intention to lead? If you don't, then you will never see the many leadership opportunities that are presented to you. Be intentional about incorporating strong leadership into your strategy.

BUILDING A POSITIVE CULTURE IN TIMES OF CHANGE

While Britney Spears made *Toxic* a major success on the dance floor, toxicity has no place in our working lives. Toxic environments affect mental and physical health, stifle innovation and creativity and can cause issues in our home life with loved ones.

I have found that workplace toxicity can gather momentum when results or goals are not being met. Everyone seems to be happy – or, at least, prepared to put up with things – when the team is winning. But when things are going south, toxic behaviour can quickly take hold.

Signs of toxicity to look out for include:

- Results not being met
- Values being compromised
- Profits being valued over customer service
- Leaders getting confused between authority and bullying
- Team communication coming to a standstill
- Inauthentic leader communication

- Passionate team members starting to become quiet and non-collaborative

- Leaders neglecting to demonstrate empathy.

Culture change must be managed through a strategic process. This is because the issues are usually more complex than leaders acknowledge, and team members might be somehow invested in upholding the status quo. As we learned in chapter 2, many of our thoughts are repetitive and negative; this is why organisational change is so hard. In my 30 years of experience with change initiatives in the corporate world I found the following four types of people (in roughly these percentages):

- **20 per cent are Change Warriors:** They want to improve and get better; they are an integral component of a leader's success in bringing about change.

- **20 per cent are Influential Resistors:** They may support change publicly, but behind closed doors will work the phones and emails to stop the change. These people are influential and heavily invested in the status quo.

- **30 per cent are Passive Resistors:** These people are not as powerful as the Influential Resistors; they are happy to consider change as long as it doesn't involve personal sacrifice.

- **30 per cent are Fence Sitters:** They believe change is logical, but have been scarred before by leaders who 'talked the talk' but never 'walked the talk', so they are not active unless there is a genuine movement.

It's important to devise a strategy for dealing with the resistors and fence sitters you might encounter along the way in achieving your vision.

PAYING FOR YOUR DREAM

Do you have a strategy for financing your dream? My personal expenditure for self-improvement is in the six figures. I have invested in travel, workshops, seminars and courses to improve myself in the pursuit of my dreams and goals. I often ask audience members at my seminars to raise their hands if they have recently invested in themselves, and hardly anyone puts their hand up. They all have dreams, goals and perhaps even a vision, but most are unwilling to spend the resources needed to better themselves. Unfortunately, these people are at risk of falling into the WCS camp: 'woulda, coulda, shoulda'.

Investment is not always about dollars: it can be about time, and other types of sacrifices. It could mean moving cities or even countries, sacrificing family time or going without holidays, fancy meals out or a new car in order to reach your bigger and better dream.

Before I won the world championship in sailing I needed to drop 7kg so that our team would be under the crew weight limit. All five of us had to work towards losing weight, and commit to each other to do this. Sometimes sacrifices are needed to achieve the bigger picture.

One of my son's school friends was given a hard time because of the quality of the car his father drove. But we knew the real story: his dad sacrificed cars and other luxuries that many people see as a necessity to list his company on the stock exchange. Now he drives his son to school in the fastest street legal Mercedes Benz, and no-one hassles his son anymore.

When I struck out to start my own business the second time there were still sacrifices, despite the fact it was my second time going in to business and I had learned so much the first time round. To build the cash flow for the business and reduce financial stress, we decided to sell two investment properties. We did not make this decision lightly, but in hindsight the sacrifice was well worth it.

Life is never a continued upward trajectory. You go up, level out, sometimes even dip a little as you invest for the future and prepare for the next growth strategy. If you look at social media, it can seem as though everyone is in an upward motion: we rarely get to see the hard work, years of sacrifice, grinding, learning and suffering before the 'overnight' success happens.

So, develop a strategy for making your dream happen, and work out your priorities and what you are willing to sacrifice. The hard work will be worth it in the end, when you achieve your vision.

STRATEGY IN ACTION

When the HP Australia leadership team asked me to take on a market development role for the commercial PC range I was naturally excited. However, I was in for a bit of a shock when I found out that HP PCs were sitting at around 15 in terms of market share. I had some work to do! I remember at one of the first meetings joking to the marketing team that we must be only just ahead of the guy who was building PCs in his backyard for the nerds playing World of Warcraft. I was even more surprised when one of the marketers said, 'Actually, that guy is at number 14'.

My first task was to find out why our dealers were not selling or stocking HP PCs. Fortunately, coming from a dealer background, I was able to get some very authentic feedback and I can assure you it was not sugar-coated. The good news was that we did not have a lot of issues. Just four. I was told our PCs were never in stock, not the right configuration and overpriced. Oh, and apparently we were also impossible to deal with. However, they did acknowledge that our product was reliable, warranty was second to none and our business model was strong.

We needed to get very creative with marketing communications and work on motivating our own people and our dealers to give us another try. One of the first things we did was empower our sales team. Our salespeople were all fantastic but were frustrated that they had to travel overseas to facilitate big deal approvals. By the time the approvals had taken place, more often than not the deal had already gone to one of our competitors. I decided to give the sales team a discretionary discount up to a certain level that they could agree to on the spot. The leadership team cautioned me, thinking I was being too trusting – but not one of the salespeople abused the privilege I gave them.

The second thing we did was focus on promoting our PCs anywhere we could. This included supplying them to Microsoft's biggest technology events so we could get our PCs in front of some of the most influential people in Australia. We could not afford TV advertising, so I did the next best thing: get our PCs onto TV sets via product placement. This led to me supplying HP PCs for major movies, including *The Matrix* trilogy. (Side note: 20 years later I met Keanu Reeves and he remembered having a HP PC thrown at him by Laurence Fishburne in a scene in *The Matrix*. You never know where your life will take you!) This TV and movie work was also very empowering for our team, which was just rewards for all the tough times that they had been through.

Here's an example of how my strategy might have looked when I was implementing this new marketing plan at HP.

Strategy document: Hewlett-Packard Commercial PCs

Vision: Elevate HP PCs to a top-five position in market share in Australia within two years

Strategy	Metric
Stock: Carry an inventory level that will allow us to sell the volume required for our desired market share.	Stock volumes, dealer orders, sales forecasting, big-deal pipeline.
Specifications: Ensure that we can design and customise our own versions of the PCs in the Australian market. In short, build a new configuration factory in Australia.	Agreement from dealers that we have the right product. Annual product road maps available before general release to ensure we could lead or match the future releases of competitors.
Pricing: Ensure we have the right pricing for the Australian market; that it is sustainable and has the commitment of our global parent.	Global sign off on our pricing strategy, agreement on funding from our parent, acknowledgement from our customers that our pricing is competitive.
Service: Be known as the most flexible, open and collaborative vendor to work with.	Rise in dealer satisfaction, dealer orders, invitations to bid.

Here are some of the gaps I identified and had to work on to fill in order to make our vision a reality:

- **Action:** We had to move quickly and with integrity. People had become impatient with HP PCs. Not only did our biggest dealers not have faith in us, but our own printer division preferred to partner with our direct competitors rather than deal with their own PC department, literally an aisle away!

- **Knowledge:** We needed some expert knowledge we did not have internally. The biggest gap in our knowledge was how to build and run a PC configuration factory. We also needed more training in leadership, management, communication and collaboration, and we had to improve our big deal bidding.

- **Process:** We needed new processes covering ordering, customisation, factory processes, variable pricing models and more.

So, what were our results? We went from number 15 in market share to inside the top 10 in six months, and then reached number two within 12 months. It was an amazing ride and I was awarded a HP High Achiever Award for the results achieved. But it was not just me; I may have led some of the marketing and communications, but the heroes were many – as is often the case with results.

FINALISING YOUR STRATEGY

By now, hopefully you have learned a few things about how to set a strategy that aligns with your vision, and some of the elements you will need to include. Once you have your strategy written down, you should do a final check to make sure it is sound.

Ask yourself:

- What impact will this strategy have on my family?

- What impact will this strategy have on my finances?

- What might this strategy require me to sacrifice?

- How do I need to prepare myself?

- How can I honour my future vision and my current responsibilities?

- What are some obstacles I need to prepare for?

6. Step 4:
Taking action

'The way you do the impossible is you take
the first possible step in front of you.'

Daniela Nica

Step 4 in the 4-Step Possibility System© is where you will start to see the magic happen. You can plan and strategise all you like, but you will never achieve your goals until you take action.

Society is so focused on labelling people as being inherently brilliant, talented and physically superior that we have duped ourselves into believing that the most valued achievements are those that are effortless. Sure, we need to identify things that we are passionate about and find easy or fun to do, but we should also recognise the scope for improving on our natural talent if we take action, push our boundaries and diligently strive to attain more. In his book *Talent Is Overrated: What Really Separates World-Class Performers from Everybody Else*, Geoff Colvin argues that deliberate effort is far more important to world-class performance than innate talent. In *Bounce: The Myth of Talent and the Power of Practice*, journalist and Olympian Matthew Syed believes that talent is not nearly as important as practice, hard work and determination for long-term success.

So let's get to it!

PUTTING THE GROWTH MINDSET INTO PRACTICE: THE CHAMPION PROCESS

To put a growth mindset into practice so it becomes a habit, I use my CHAMPION process. I have used this process to achieve massive change and to obtain goals that were a stretch for me but worthwhile.

C   **Chunk** it down

H   **Have** a go

A   **Assess** your results

M   **Mindset** maintenance

P   Hang out with the right **people**

I   **Investigate** the best

O   **Own** the outcome

N   **Never** give in

Chunk it down

Many of my clients overestimate what they can achieve in 12 months, yet underestimate what they can achieve in three years. Very often they have a well-thought-out, achievable goal, but give up on it because they didn't achieve it in the unrealistic time frame they allocated to it. One way to avoid this is to break the goal down into manageable chunks, which can be completed before moving on to the next one.

I have found a great way to chunk down goals is via a mind map. You will be surprised how effective a visual map can be to show progress towards a worthwhile goal.

Have a go

Before I began cycling, I had always considered doing a race but knew nothing about the actual sport. I wanted to compete in a criterium race, as it looked intriguing – especially the tactics and the final sprint. (In a criterium or 'crit' race, you ride for a set time around a short course. As you begin the last lap, a bell rings and then it's on for young and old – not surprisingly, this is when the most crashes occur.) When I was discussing my desire to do a crit 'one day' with one of my cycling colleagues, she said, 'Well, you'll never know unless you give it a go'.

One of the best things about organised events such as races is that there is a start time. You either show up, or you don't. No-one is waiting for you. One of my friends once told me that he likes boat racing because it forces you to have a go, no matter what the conditions are like out on the water. It's not like cruising, where you might stay in port for a few days waiting for the perfect conditions before sailing to the next port; when you race, you show up for the start and get on with it, and learn to adapt to conditions as you go.

Having a go doesn't mean you necessarily need to compete, but it does mean you need to get out and try. Positive thinking is great, but positive *doing* is when the magic happens.

Having a go means not just having a go once; you need to keep having a go, again and again, learning each time and noting your progress. Think back to when you learned to ride a bike, drive a car, ride a motorcycle, surf, or play netball or basketball. It took effort and repetition, and only with persistence were you able to master the activity. You were persistent then, so you know you can do it this time too.

Having a go can also relate to generating ideas for your business, if you are an entrepreneur. Blogger, entrepreneur and author James Altucher says ideas are the new currency, but you have to come up with them. He advises taking action by thinking of 10 new ideas a day. These ideas may not even have to be for you – they could be for someone else. It's the practice of idea generation that is your gain. Stand-up comedians know that to be successful they have to continually write jokes. Good or bad, it doesn't matter – it's the creative process carried out repetitively that drives the learning. Some comedians hold themselves and their comedy friends accountable by writing 10 jokes a day and emailing them to each other.

For those of you in school or university there are so many opportunities to expand your mindset and experiences. But nothing will happen if you don't have a go. In my senior year at school I was in the Australian Army Cadets – a community-based youth development program based on the Army's customs, traditions and values. I held a junior leadership position of Lance Corporal, which at my school was regarded as a consolation prize for those not good enough to be Corporal. Despite feeling like I was in a lowly position, I let one of my cadet friends, Chris Carra, talk me in to completing the Platoon Commander Course. I tried to tell him he was nuts – I was a lowly Lance Corporal, while he was already a Sergeant. But Chris would have none of it. He convinced me to have a go, despite the fact that the course was way above my skill level and current capability. After the course was over, I had to face the facts and the selection committee. We all sat around at a campsite (think *Survivor*) and one by one were called by the selection committee to be notified whether we passed, failed or were expelled for incompetence. When it came my time, I nervously made the walk to the committee desperately hoping I would not have to face the embarrassment of going home with the same rank as I started with. Sure enough, the committee told me that I was on the program only because someone else had dropped out and they needed even numbers. But then they said that, despite the odds, I had actually passed and even excelled in several areas so they had no choice but to make me a Platoon Commander. In that course, and the following year in my role as

Platoon Commander, I gained more leadership experience than I did in the next 10 years in business. I'm so grateful to my friend, Chris, for pushing me to see what was possible and encouraging me to have a go. He was one of the earliest examples of a Possibility Leader I was lucky enough to meet.

When my youngest son, Lachie, was in grade three, he decided that he wanted to sing a solo at his primary school Christmas break up. His song of choice was Madonna's *Like a Prayer* – a bit of a controversial number for his relatively conservative school. While Lachie had a great voice for such a young boy, as a professional speaker I knew how intimidating it could be to get in front of a big audience for the first time. While I was very supportive of him (I have always encouraged my kids to 'have a go'), I did have some niggling concerns. So, I worked with Lachie, his teacher and the school principal to put a strategy together for the big day, and helped Lachie develop a rehearsal plan (i.e. we chunked the vision down). But I knew, no matter how much rehearsal we did or how intentional Lachie was with his groundwork, nothing could fully prepare him for the experience of walking out in front of his entire school and parents to sing. This would have to be his own, unique experience and it is impossible to get it any other way than to have a go! Lachie ended up doing a great job and loved it so much that now, some eight years later, he still sings. Parents – sometimes we worry *way* too much.

Assess your results

There has never been a truer saying than 'what gets measured gets done'. When we know what we are aiming at and how we're tracking its so much easier to achieve our goals. Metrics need to be clear, concise and easy to assess. I also believe in transparency: you should share your metrics with a coach or mentor so they can keep you honest about how you are going. The same applies with teams: that is why the scoreboard is such a great measure in sport.

My favourite strategy to assess results is the acronym KFC (no, this is not to do with Colonel Sanders!):

K   **Know** what you want specifically

F   **Find** out if you are achieving it regularly

C   **Change** what's not working quickly

This is impossible to do without metrics. Luckily, today there is simply no excuse for a lack of metrics. We have access to more data than ever before, and we should use this to our advantage. Take, for example, my cycling story in the introduction to the book. Every time I go for a ride I am collecting the following data:

- Heart rate
- Watts (pressure on the pedals)
- Cadence (how fast I am spinning the pedals)
- Calorie burn
- Distance
- Altitude
- Speed
- Location of ride
- Ride time
- Overall effort.

(This is just for a practice ride – not even a race!)

Metrics are an integral part of sport. You know whether you won or lost, or whether you improved on your personal best. For some reason, metrics seem less important and not as well understood when you move from sport to business and personal development. I can't tell you how many large organisations I work with who can't explain the metrics they are tracking. Without this information it is quite difficult to know which interventions to suggest, because it is unclear how the organisation is currently performing.

If you come up with a metric, make sure you can actually measure it. Once, when I was working with a large bank, the strategists came up with a new metric they wanted to measure. It made sense, it was logical and it was timely. The only problem was: no-one knew how to calculate it on a regular basis. It became worse than useless, as the bankers would guess the measurement or use a variety of different methods to calculate it, meaning their data was unreliable.

So many people want to make the magic million dollars per year, but don't actually put in any effort to think of how they might measure their progress towards this goal. Here is an example some of my internet marketing colleagues use. One million can be made by:

- Selling 5000 × $200 solutions
- Selling 250 × $4000 Solutions
- Having 5000 people pay you $17 per month for 12 months
- Having 250 people pay you $334 per month for 12 months

You can play with these numbers and go further into weekly and daily figures, which I would encourage you to do if you want to measure the detail.

The world's most-recognised high-performance companies such as General Electric, Amazon, Google, Apple and the like all use metrics to define strategies, but also use metrics to signal when to abandon their strategy or implement changes if they go off track. We can all do the same thing, whether it be in our work or personal life.

What I also like about metrics and data is that they bring confidence. When you measure things, you find evidence that can often back up your 'gut feel'. Data is also excellent when you are coaching someone or wanting to instigate a change within a team. Data takes the subjectivity out of the discussion because everyone is looking at the same facts. It prevents wild opinions, and especially quietens those people who love to view their opinions as fact. As a skill the ability to understand, interpret and interrogate data is something needed in future jobs. Generation Y and Z have a jump start on us as they have been brought up on data. My sons, for example, know all about their followers on Instagram. They know the percentage of followers and likes from which country and when they experience the highest engagement. This data allows them to optimise when they post content so they can capitalise on times of strong engagement.

I use the following acronym, taught to me by a fellow coach, when I am assessing my results after a race or business event:

WWW   What went well?

EBI   Even better if?

NT   Next time?

AU   All up?

(To help me remember it, I think of it as a website address: www. ebi.nt.au.)

Mindset maintenance

We spoke about mindset in chapter 3 as the first step in the 4-Step Possibility System©. But it's not just a matter of getting your mindset right once and then forgetting about it. As you take action, you must continually reevaluate your mindset and make sure you are still on track.

Motivational speaker Les Brown's words have gotten me out of a few tight spots when my mindset has gone off track. Les says we must keep working every day, every week on keeping our mindset healthy and positive, so that we are prepared for when tough times come, or when an opportunity presents itself and we need to step up. Les suggests we spend around 40 minutes a day reinforcing our mindset with positive messages.

Once I was at the airport about to fly to Asia to run a series of business development workshops when I had a call from my US business partner. He advised me that a key influencer in one of my largest accounts had contacted him, and they wanted to remove me from the account. This was quite a shock. There had been no history of any issues, and no communication directly to me. It was a major issue, as this account represented some 50 per cent of my income at the time – and as I was a business owner, I didn't have a salary to fall back on. To the absolute credit of my US colleague, he did not accept the client's request on face value; instead, he insisted on a consultative approach to find out what the issue was, so that if I was replaced there would be learnings that could be applied in the future. It was a good strategy; however, I can tell you it is impossible to avoid taking this kind of situation personally and start questioning almost everything you do.

The worst part about the situation was that it made me feel very down about myself right before I had to be the upbeat positive energy in the room delivering a new workshop. Not ideal. I knew that, as a performer of sorts, I would bring my energy to the room and the audience would be able to feel it right away. So, I knew it was important to get my mindset back on track to be my best for my next audience. I immediately set about using all the tricks I knew to get the positive vibes flowing again, and ended up listening to a motivational speech by Les Brown in an attempt to pull myself back up. Les said: 'Someone's opinion of you does not need to define you'. It was just what I needed to hear, and the workshop went very well.

Oh, and I did end up retaining my big account. The issue turned out to be political, with one person trying to secure a stronger role for themselves in the client's business. The lessons I learned from this experience were:

- Don't have 50 per cent of your business with one client

- People are motivated for personal reasons before business reasons

- It's never really about you personally – it usually has more to do with what the other person is looking to achieve (sometimes you are just the collateral damage)

- Mindset maintenance can help you see this perspective and keep you focused for all the clients, friends and family who do value you.

The battle in your mind can be tough at times, and must be fought with the intention and discipline of a warrior.

Hang out with the right people

In my opinion, motivation is 50 per cent ourselves and 50 per cent the people we hang out with. When I decided to pursue sales performance advisory and sales leader training I aligned with the gold standard at the time, the US based company Miller Heiman. I met several fantastic consultants who were all keen to assist me. However, they all told me that I would only ever sell a maximum of $1 million worth of consulting and training services each year. In fact, they told me, the highest anyone from Australia had achieved was US$750 000 in one year. I firmly believe that, when you impose a lid on something (even if it is a fact), you close down the possibility of 'what might be'. And that's not how I operate.

I decided to fly to the US (at my own expense) to connect with the American leadership team at Miller Heiman, to deepen my knowledge and learn new skills from the best in the business. More importantly, I wanted to make sure my attitude and mind-set were aligned to the global best. While I was there, I was lucky enough to connect with two outstanding consultants: Rob West and Kathy Nelson. Both had set new sales records working with some of the world's most respected brands. This was a whole new level of thinking for me, and something that was just not available back in Australia at the time. Rob and Kathy were selling around 10 times more than the best in Australia. This visit to the US opened up a whole new world of possibility for me that I had been told was impossible.

I continued my dialogue with Rob and Kathy on my return and they introduced me to others who had a no limits approach: people such Tom Williams (co-author of the excellent book *The Seller's Challenge*) and oil industry guru Mickey O'Callaghan.

A few months after my return, one of my old bosses from my dotcom start-up days, Bill Lang, asked me what I knew about sales processes and improving sales performance on a big scale. 'Well, let me tell you, Bill!' I thought. Long story short, I partnered with Bill, encouraged him to align with Miller Heiman and we secured a big contract with one of Australia's largest banks. In my second year with Miller Heiman, my total revenue in for the company was around US$5.5 million. This catapulted me to global number one consultant that year, narrowly edging out my mentor Rob West.

The take-out is this: if your current network of friends, family or work colleagues is not supporting you and encouraging you to grow, you will never have the opportunity to be who you could be. You need to seek out those who believe in your dream and can encourage and guide you on your journey there.

The same applies to sport. Global sporting app Strava found that when riders cycled in groups rather than alone they rode an average of 52 per cent longer in distance. They also found that when riders slowed down or stopped during a ride they were able to get back up to speed faster when they cycled in a group.[9]

The only caveat when you are hanging out with people you are comfortable with is to be wary of getting *too* comfortable. There is a wise quote that says, 'If you are the fastest person in your team you need to get a new team'. The same applies if you are the smartest person in your group or organisation.

A good friend of mine was a very fast Porsche race driver. He was complaining that the members of his current club were holding him back, challenging his aggressiveness on the track and disapproving of modifications he had made to his car. When he asked for my advice, I told him that he was the problem, not them. I told him he had outgrown his current club and he needed to step up and race at a more professional level. His current people were not going to grow to the level he aspired to, and he had to respect that. He took my advice on board and not only did he step up, he actually won the higher-level series.

Questions to ask along the way

- What can I start doing now?
- Are there any creative actions I haven't considered?
- What markers or indicators can I use that will help me in the early action stage?
- Who is doing something similar who might inspire me?
- How do I feel as I am taking action towards my vision?
- What is something I would be willing to do knowing I won't win or be the best, but will learn a tremendous amount?

Investigate the best

Once you have a goal or dream and are committed to it, part of your strategy should be to find out who does it best in the world and study them. If you live in Australia like me, this might mean taking some overseas trips.

Former Rugby Union Australian captain Stirling Mortlock once told me that his strategy is to find out who is the best in the world in what he wants to do, and then practise until he perfects it. He doesn't try to argue with the person's method or change how they do things to suit himself. He says that when you have reached world-class, that's when you have earned the right to change it up.

When I was in sailing, my good friend Stuart Wallace won the 1986 World Laser Championships and countless other competitions. When Stuart decided to sell his boat to focus on cycling (a passion we both share), I bought it off him – figuring it would eliminate my excuses when racing. When I rigged Stuart's boat it was set up very differently to mine – I really struggled with how Stuart had set up his ropes and knots. I was so tempted to change things to make them the way I thought they should be, but I resisted the temptation – Stuart had been world champion and I wanted to learn from him. So I persevered, asked Stuart for his advice and found that, after I had developed my technique and skills to a higher level, the setup of ropes and knots Stuart had provided me with was perfect.

'Don't wish it was easier;
wish you were better.'

Jim Rohn

When I intentionally switched from sailing to cycling I knew, despite many years of motorcycle riding, that I had serious knowledge gaps. I could fill these gaps myself, or I could call on experts and world-class professionals to teach me. The latter has been a practice of mine forever. I would always seek out the best and learn from them, either by working for them, working with them, studying under them or having them as part of my team as a coach. The reason this is a great strategy is that anyone who is successful in life, be it in business, sport or any other area, is always passionate about what they do – and nine times out of 10, they will be happy to share what they know with someone who is equally as passionate but not yet as skilled.

Own the outcome

If you want to become a true Possibility Leader, you must always take active responsibility for your actions – whatever the result. If you get a positive result, be happy for yourself for putting in all the effort and work that went into it. Don't play it down, and don't let anyone steal the glory. But, if it all goes horribly wrong, don't look for someone to blame. Take responsibility, admit your error and then get on with locking down the learning and move on. Authenticity is vital; people will respect you for it. Everyone makes mistakes, so own the outcome no matter what it is. (This is also an important lesson to teach your team, or your children if you are a parent. We all need to be responsible for our actions.)

In 1986 I was competing in the J24 Class World Championships in Newport, Rhode Island. I had trouble with a charter boat I had secured, in that it wasn't as described in the brochure, so I had to find a better boat with only a few days' notice. US and current world champion Ken Read heard of my plight, and despite not knowing me well offered his raceboat to me and my crew to get some practice in. It was an amazing gesture given Ken had a lot more to lose out of this, given he was the hot favourite. However, it turns out I misunderstood the timing Ken had allowed for me, and while I had the boat Ken was needing to work on it with his crew. To say it was an interesting greeting back at the dock would be an understatement. I apologised to Ken and took full responsibility, asking how I could make it up to him. Rightly, he said I could start by completing the work on the boat that he and his crew were planning, which was preparing the bottom of the hull. I agreed, and that's what I did. It was a tough, tiring job but I had made the error, so I had to follow through. Ken inspected it later that day, told me he was surprised I even did it and then he went on to win that world championship. A few years later I partnered with Ken to win his sixth and my first world championship in this class. Taking ownership for your actions will serve you, every time, in one way or another.

Another time I was sailing in my second Melbourne to Devonport race across Bass Strait. I had a good team and we sailed well, but we made a navigation error and got the current wrong. We ended up third overall, but it was disappointing given we sailed for much longer and in tougher conditions than we needed to. Even though I was not the navigator, I was the skipper and it was my responsibility to make sure we had the navigation right. So, I owned it. The first thing I did was sit down with the navigator and we worked out our error together.

The following year we entered again, and I took the same navigator because the last thing I wanted was for some other boat to gain from what we had learned through our mistake the previous year. I also took time to meet with the winning skipper from the previous year, Rohan Simpson, who helped with some key ideas on how to best sail the race. We entered again, and this time we won. I was the youngest skipper to win the race at that time. I was really happy for the owner of the boat, Peter Goodman, who had put his faith in me. The point is: it's just as important to own the outcome when it goes wrong as it is when it goes right.

Many people would have heard of Olympic Gold Medallist speed skater Steven Bradbury, who won the gold when all his fellow skaters crashed in front of him on the last lap. In Australia, when you win something by default, people often say you 'Did a Bradbury'. This is terribly unfair to Steven. What most people don't know is that Steven had to first qualify to be eligible for the Olympics. Then he had to make it to the final. His strategy of hanging back and waiting for other mistakes to happen actually got him into the final. So, in the final, he thought: 'Why change the winning strategy?'. In the final, as things really heated up, he was at the back and yes, his competitors all took themselves out and Steven cruised over the line to victory. When he was collecting his medal he did question whether he deserved it, given he didn't win it for outright speed. But he quickly changed his mind (rightly so) and claimed the gold medal as a reward not for that race, but for the years and years of training, injuries and sacrifices he had made to get there. Steven owned the outcome.

Never give in

Kacey Musgraves won the album of the year at the 2019 Grammy Awards, but it hasn't all been a walk in the park for her. *Billboard* listed Kacey's song *Follow Your Arrow* at number two on their list of 20 Best Songs of 2013, yet at the 2013 Country Music Awards the famous line 'roll up a joint' was censored, because it was deemed too controversial for primetime television. *Follow Your Arrow* received mixed reviews from conservative Americans who claimed the country tune was 'an attack on Christians'. Kacey worked through the difficulties, saying she has 'just wanted to be herself' from day one – even if it means having 10 listeners rather than 10 000.

Lady Gaga (Stefani Germanotta) always wanted to be an actress before becoming a singer and songwriter. This is what makes her role in the award-winning movie *A Star is Born* even more important. While Bradley Cooper was keen to cast her in the lead role due to her powerful voice, songwriting credentials and their chemistry, unfortunately, Warner Bros., which was financing the film, did not agree. Bradley had to shoot several screen tests with Lady Gaga to convince them she could play Ally, the undiscovered singer who is the 'star' of the film. Lady Gaga went on to be nominated for best female lead and win best original song at the 2019 Academy Awards. She is quoted as saying: 'It's not about how many times you get rejected, fall down or get beaten, it's about how many times you stand up, be brave and keep on going'.

SOMETIMES YOU WIN, SOMETIMES YOU LEARN

One of the fastest ways of diving in to action is to free yourself from concerns about the result, and focus on how much you might learn.

When I decided to take cycling a little more seriously, I wondered how I could collapse time and learn everything I wanted to know in a very condensed time frame. The answer was the World Masters Games in Auckland in 2017. This event was to be held 18 months after I first pulled on the cycling lycra. I had sailed in the World Masters Games in Sydney so knew that while it was a serious event it was not as intense as the UCI World Championships. However, it would be a huge step for me.

I told a few friends of my goal and was laughed at. I told a few cycling store assistants and they, too, were sceptical. But they didn't know I was not going there to win; I was going to learn. To learn to the maximum effect, I had to eliminate as many variables as possible. I researched and bought a great bike and hired

Australian Olympic cyclist and Giro d'Italia stage winner Matty Lloyd as my coach.

The first time I met Matty we agreed to meet at a coffee shop, and then go for a ride so he could assess if I had any major technique issues. When I greeted Matty he said: 'Great to meet you, and Dad says hi'. It turns out, Matty's father is world and Australian sailing champion and Sydney to Hobart winner Ross Lloyd, who I had the great pleasure of racing with many times. (It's a small world so always be kind.)

Matty wrote me a program, corrected some technique issues and got me going in the right direction. He is a real champion and was very supportive of this newbie to a sport that was his profession, and one he had been world-class in. One thing I will never forget was riding along Beach Road in Melbourne – a popular cycling road – with Matty and him telling me how important it is to ride slowly to build strength and technique, as other riders rode past us having no clue who they were passing (not me; Matty!).

I bought cycling magazines, I watched YouTube, I read books by Cadel Evans, Robbie McEwen and others (which all helped) and I underlined parts and made notes in my journal. But as I was soon to learn, there is a big difference between knowledge and skill.

After some practice, race day came and we arrived at the course some 30km from Auckland's CBD. At this point, my normally very supportive wife Leisa said, 'Rob, are you sure you are at the right event? These guys look ... well ... very professional'. Not very helpful or confidence-building, but I had to admit I was feeling the same way – well out of my league.

When the race started I decided to begin towards the back so I could hide in the peloton until I was ready, as Robbie McEwen suggested. Well, that's a good idea if you can ride as fast as the peloton. And did I mention it was still pitch black, and when the starter said 'go' it started pouring with rain? So much for my strategy.

When we hit the first major climb I was spent by the top, but fortunately my motorcycle riding experience kicked in and I was reasonably quick on the descents. After the first lap, an experienced rider who was coaching a couple of people pulled a motley crew of us together and we rode as a team for the next seven laps of the road circuit. I survived the wet and even had enough energy combined with adrenaline to have a sprint for the finish.

I finished around midfield in my age group, which I was very pleased with. When I got back to my car, I asked the guy packing up near me (who had finished an outstanding third) what he was doing prior to the race. He looked at me like I was either an idiot, completely naïve or real newbie. (Actually, I think I was all three.) But not only did he explain why you have to warm up, he described what your body needs to be able to race competitively and then reassembled his wind trainer and bike and showed me his setup. I was so grateful for his generosity, but still very aware that knowledge doesn't equal skill – I was going to have to put everything I learned into practice if I had any hope of success in this new sport.

DON'T MAKE THE 'WOULDA-COULDA-SHOULDA' MISTAKE

A few years back I was at a sailing regatta and the guest of honour was Olympic Gold Medallist in the 470 Sailing Class, Tom King. Tom learned to sail on his parents' dam, then progressed to the seaside town of Inverloch and then to Albert Park Lake. After much local success he won two world championships and then a gold medal. Tom is a man of action. However, despite all these credentials, while Tom was talking about his passion for the sport a couple of guys behind me in the crowd were discussing how they were easily as good as Tom and they both remember beating him in races in his early days. They went on to say that if only work, family, mortgages and life hadn't got in the way, they could have easily been like Tom. That was enough for me. I turned around and asked them politely to be quiet, as I was keen to listen to someone who pursued his dreams with action rather than two people with 'woulda-coulda-shoulda' strategies. That made them shut up!

So, the lesson here is be open to learning. Ask questions, be authentic, be honest, be curious be grateful but above all please have a go!

PART III
THE ACTION PROCESS

'One day you will wake up and
there won't be any more time to
do the things you've always wanted.
Do it now.'

Paulo Coelho

7. Building knowledge

'One of the greatest gifts you can give yourself,
right here, right now, is to decide, without apology,
to commit to the journey, and not to the outcome.'

Joyce DiDonato

As you start taking action to achieve your vision you will most likely encounter some gaps in your knowledge and skills that you will need to address. You might already have identified some of these and worked out how to acquire them while you were putting together your strategy in chapter 5. Others might not come up until you start putting your strategy into action.

BE STRATEGIC

It's important to be strategic and realistic about which of your knowledge gaps need to be filled, and how.

A few years ago, as part of a Certified Practising Accountants (CPA) roadshow, I had the pleasure of interviewing Wotif founder Graeme Wood. Graeme told me that after he came up with his concept for his business he realised he would need to improve his internet skills so he could explain his concept to IT professionals. Rather than hire experts to do this, Graeme went back to school. He learned how to code to a level at which he was able build a prototype of the Wotif ebusiness. This not only allowed him to show his concept and design to the IT professionals he needed to build the site to a world-class level, but it also provided him with credibility so he wouldn't be ripped off by his developers.

When I moved from accounting into IT business development I was completely out of my depth with all the technical jargon, anacronyms and constant new technology updates. What I *did* know was how to navigate corporate structures. I decided that I could spend countless hours studying technology, or I could focus on what I was good at (understanding people and organisations) and leave the technical side to those who were qualified in that area. My thinking was that technology would always change, but people didn't; I learned just enough about technology that I could advise customers and confidently assess when I needed to defer to someone more qualified.

This strategy paid off in a way I did not expect. I found that I became well respected by the technical team, because I brought them into conversations and opportunities before the sale, rather than afterwards when it was too late for them to provide valuable feedback. My way was a partnership approach, which I thought was logical – but apparently I was only one of a few who did this.

You might find that it is best for your business to defer to others who have specialist knowledge in the area you are lacking, rather than trying to become an expert in every single area yourself. And your team might appreciate it, too!

HOW FAR WOULD YOU GO FOR KNOWLEDGE?

'When all hope seems lost and you're sitting in the wreckage of your attempts, remember you are defying your destiny through the courage of your intent.'

Fiori Giovanni

Fiori Giovanni is a friend of mine and a fellow speaker and coach. Her story makes most of our lives seem like fairytales. At the age of 12, Fiori's marriage was already arranged. If that is not horrifying enough, at 14 she was recruited to fight in the Eritrean Army. Her destiny, like that of so many other girls in developing nations, had been dictated, defined and determined. It was yet, though, to be defied. Her decision-makers, including the Eritrean Army, had not realised the strength of her will.

At the ripe old age of 15 years, Fiori made the harrowing decision to flee war-torn Eritrea without friends or family. She crossed five continents and 20 countries in search of knowledge, personal growth and wisdom. This journey eventually led her to settle in Australia, where she's now a highly sought-after keynote speaker and a respected business and executive coach. As a result of repeatedly overcoming harrowing life experiences and insurmountable obstacles, Fiori has decoded her steps towards survival, transformation and success, creating a formula that empowers others to overcome their own problems, no matter how big or small.

THE ULTIMATE KNOWLEDGE GAP: CHANGING CAREERS

I have changed careers many times. I think I am ahead of the curve here, as I believe many people will require this skill in the workplace of the future. Here are the careers I've held over 35 years:

- Motor mechanic
- Accountant at KPMG, Rio Tinto and Kraft
- Business to business sales manager at an Apple reseller
- Channel manager at Apple
- Strategic marketing development manager at Hewlett-Packard
- Global advertising agency executive at Publicis Mojo
- Small business marketing consultant
- Global sales performance adviser
- Global leadership speaker.

Along the way I have also had side hustles in:

- Photography
- Music and entertainment
- Radio and podcasting
- TV.

Each time I have changed careers I have been prepared to pay the price by investing in myself, to develop the additional knowledge

I would need. (As it's often said, if you are good at spotting a wise investment you should know you need to invest in yourself first.)

A good example of this was my shift from IT to a global advertising agency. First, I decided on my goal: to work for a HP-size business and brand, but in the advertising world rather than IT. I knew that, to show my future employer I was serious, I would have to put in some effort to learn my craft, so I joined a smaller marketing agency first – figuring I would get a better look at the entire business, since the team was quite small and everyone was involved in all parts of the chain. Once I had ticked off several years in the smaller business, I felt I had filled my knowledge gap sufficiently to apply for a global agency role.

That time I stood in for Mike Myers

In late 1999 I was keen to enhance my speaking skills and the way I presented, so I decided to take a stand-up comedy course. This would encompass comedy writing and performing, and I hoped I would learn interesting techniques such as rehearsed spontaneity. I enrolled in a program run by legendary comedian Pete Crofts at his Humourversity.

At the time, the Austin Powers movie had just been released and I thought it hilarious – I especially loved the flawed character Dr Evil. The roles of both Austin Powers and Dr Evil were played by the very talented Mike Myers, who also wrote and produced the movie.

Anyway, one day at Humourversity I was reciting some of Dr Evil's famous lines when one of my co-participants said, 'Hey, that's pretty good. Want to have a go doing it for real?'. He introduced himself as Tom Spalding, the lead singer of Melbourne rock band Captain Spalding. Tom explained that he had put together a show based around the music and characters of the Austin Powers movie, but he didn't yet have a Dr Evil performer. He asked if I would like to audition.

Once again I set off on a new chapter of my life and jumped in off the deep end. I have to say that Tom Spalding is a very good salesperson, too. He invited me to play the Dr Evil role, but he didn't mention that it was a full-on live rock'n'roll show and I had to learn to sing two songs as well as MC the night and do some comedy during costume changes. I had never sung, and while I love music I am not very good with timing. For nearly three years of performing with the band I would always start my songs with my back to the audience, looking for the keyboard player Billy to say 'now!'. Then I would turn around and start my song. From here I was asked by a group of dancers who had an Austin Powers routine playing at Crown Casino to play the Dr Evil role midweek. I managed to bring together the Captain Spalding Band and the dancers in a corporate gig for Optus. Tom and I even went on to appear for Village Roadshow at the launch of the *Austin Powers 2* DVD and *Austin Powers 3* when Mike Myers was unable to make it to Australia.

Through all of this I learned more about stage craft and audience interaction from Tom and the band than I could ever have learned on my own. I continue to put what I learned into practise at my speaking gigs today.

LEARN ABOUT YOUR BEHAVIOURAL STYLE

We all have our personal ways of behaving in different situations. We tend to act routinely, repeating our adapted ways of doing things because it is easier to do this than to learn new ways. Our brain is constantly attempting to predict situations and make meaning according to what we have experienced before, which is why we tend to form an opinion of another person almost immediately – whether we want to or not.

It's important to understand your behavioural style (and those of your team members) when you are working towards a vision or goal. This knowledge will help you communicate and relate effectively with others, as well as giving you insights into how you might best motivate yourself to achieve your goals.

I have used the Extended DISC model for the past 10 years, and have found it invaluable for my growth. DISC is based on the work of William Moulton Marston (who, incidentally, also created the comic book character Wonder Woman). It stands for:

D Dominance
I Influence
S Steadiness
C Compliance

The diagram overleaf shows the four Extended DISC elements and the perceived positives and negatives of each. A DISC assessment will help you work out which quadrant you fall into.

It's important to remember that the DISC model is a tool for observing and analysing *behaviour*, not *personality*. The model does not classify people as good or bad, nor does it measure intelligence, emotional intelligence, knowledge or skills. None of the behavioural styles is better or worse than the other; they all have their benefits and challenges. The key is to understand your own style and the effect your behaviour may have on others. If you lead a team, DISC is a fantastic way for all team members to learn about each other's behavioural preferences. You will achieve your goal far more quickly if your team respects each others' talents and abilities.

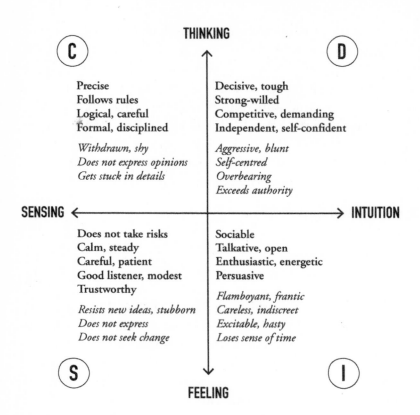

DISC also helps me in my personal relationships, and I have brought my wife, Leisa, and our children on board. (It is suitable to use with young people from the age when they can comprehend the words used in the questionnaire.) In the DISC programs I favour, such as Extended DISC and the Maxwell Method of DISC, you can obtain a work pair or team analysis – which is very insightful for couples and people who need to work closely together. Over the years, Leisa and I have seen our natural styles shift to complement each other. My natural profile is D/I and Leisa is S/I, and because we understand this we are able to leverage each others' natural strengths for the benefit of us both.

Some final words on DISC:

- DISC is a behavioural inventory based on self-evaluation. It describes your natural reaction mode or behavioural style in different situations.

- DISC does not classify people as 'good' or 'bad', give high or low scores or limit a person's ability to develop in another direction or work environment.

- Less than 1 per cent of people are a pure D, I, S or C; most people are a combination of two or three styles.

- We can shift our natural behavior over time around the diamond but typically not significantly.

- I recommend this not be a 'do it once' assessment. You should complete an assessment every 12 months, if possible, to review you natural and adjusted styles.

LEARN ABOUT YOUR HEALTH

I am a big believer in both the physical and mental benefits of exercise. Many people don't get to start or see their dreams through because they run out of one or more of three things:

- Time
- Health
- Money.

I used to think that time was the greatest asset, until I spoke to a group of retirees and they set me straight: health, they said, was the greatest asset, and they all wished they had been more proactive at managing their health earlier in life.

So many of us start gym memberships, buy gym equipment, buy a bike, do a retreat or enter a race but never see it through.

It is amazing the excuses we come up with as to why we can't focus on our health right now. Here are few chestnuts from my own extensive library:

- Work
- Travel
- Kids
- Parents
- Relatives
- Illness
- Too cold

- Too hot
- I was tired
- Big night
- Early morning
- Bike broke down
- Car broke down
- *I* broke down.

Some people will tell you that if you are using all these excuses it must be because your 'why' isn't compelling enough. But I think there is another angle: that is, you just don't enjoy the activity you have chosen. Honestly, I don't enjoy the gym. I don't enjoy running and I don't enjoy exercise bikes, but I love to ride outdoors. Road bike, mountain bike, time trial, BMX – I don't care, I just like being on two wheels. It's not exercise, its fun! Even the former First Lady, Michelle Obama, agrees with me on this: she once said that if you can find a sport or activity that you really enjoy doing, it won't seem like exercise at all.

So go on: think outside the box, and come up with a strategy for finding a sport or exercise you actually enjoy. It will make it 100 times easier to haul yourself out of bed on a chilly Sunday morning – I promise.

Exercise for your brain

A study by the University of Illinois found that regular exercise can improve memory and learning.[10] The study found that daily cycling increased participants' hippocampus by 2 per cent and improved their memory and problem-solving skills by 15 to

20 per cent after six months. The cyclists reported a greater ability to focus and an improved attention span. Also, their brains appeared two years younger than their non-exercising peers.

Exercise can also have a positive effect on mental health. When we exercise, serotonin rises in our body (giving us a post-exercise glow); dopamine spikes, which sharpens our focus and speeds up muscle reaction times; the body pumps out norepinephrine, allowing us to process information at a subconscious level (ever had a breakthrough thought while exercising?); and we increase cannabinoid, giving us a natural burst of euphoria.

I carry a phone with me on rides – not so much for emergencies, but for putting all the ideas that have popped up during the ride into the 'notes' app when I stop for the mandatory coffee. Next time you exercise, notice how many brilliant ideas you have (and how many jobs you remember that you need to do). It is very motivating.

If Aaron can, you can

I met Aaron Wood at a public relations masterclass run by Kate Engler. Kate asked us to pair up and discuss our offer to the market. I went first, telling Aaron about what I did, why I was passionate about it and where I was going. Then it was Aaron's turn.

Aaron is a personal trainer, but his road to fitness came from necessity. Being born with an incurable terminal illness, he didn't have much wriggle room. He qualified as a personal trainer at the age of 18 and said he has never looked back since.

Aaron started his personal training business with the goal of inspiring and sharing his experience and passion with others. Since then, he has had the privilege of making real differences in people's lives, helping them to reach their goals and develop a passion for health and fitness.

Aaron said that while he may never be cured, he wouldn't stop fighting and passing on his passion for health and fitness. He said that no matter what you are going through in life, a healthy lifestyle can make you feel better, look better and give you the strength you need to fight any battles you may come across.

When Aaron finished telling me his story, I almost hugged him – but we had only just met, so I resisted. (We hugged on day two!)

Aaron spends a lot of his time motivating men and women around my age to experience the benefits of physical fitness. The number one reason, he says, is to be around to see children and grandchildren grow up. Aaron is amazing and a true positive spirit making a difference in the world.

Nutrition

Even if you're not a sportsperson, it's important to take stock of what you are fuelling yourself with. Understanding and implementing a strategy for good nutrition will help you have more energy, better concentration levels and the ability to recover quickly from any health-related setbacks.

When I was preparing for the world championships in sailing, I knew for me to be eligible to compete I needed to drop my weight to 68kg. This meant losing 6kg. I had to limit dairy and sugar as much as I could, which was quite tricky with a full life and travel on my agenda – not to mention my sweet tooth! However, if your 'why' is big enough you will always find a way.

Recently I started taking nutrition more seriously and bought some books and guides to see what I could improve on. The problem was, I was out of my depth and needed expertise. My myopathy and physiotherapy specialist connected me with Steph Lowe: known as the Natural Nutritionist and author of *Low Carb Healthy Fat Nutrition: Supercharge Your Metabolism, Burn Fat and Extend Your Longevity*. Steph is also a triathlete and cyclist, so she understands my goals and motivation. Steph shared some basic guidelines that have served me well:

- Focus on food that comes out of the ground, off a tree or from an animal
- Significantly reduce packaged food consumption
- Try to avoid gluten, refined sugars and trans fats where possible
- Include a good amount of healthy fats in my diet, plus protein and carbohydrates.

Nutrition is a very individual thing depending your health, age, activity and goals, so I encourage you to find your own expert who can provide specific guidance for you and help you design a strategy for your nutrition. I can tell you from experience that it is quite amazing what is possible with activity and a personal nutrition plan. I was able to drop weight and not only feel better, but have more energy than I did 15 years earlier. Be aware, though, this kind of change can be expensive – in that you may need a new wardrobe. Good news if you like shopping, like I do!

TAKE CHARGE OF YOUR OWN LEARNING

I have been fortunate to see how organisations such as Intrepid Learning, Telstra, Samsung and Microsoft train their staff. As you would expect, these large organisations understand that acquiring knowledge is a big deal, and they provide quality online and face-to-face training for their employees.

But these days, you don't need to rely on your employer for your learning and development. There are new ways to learn using technology, and you can access world-class tutors and content with just the click of your mouse – often for free. (This is what I call 'just in time learning', and it is much more effective than 'just in case learning', where you might be required to sit through a year-long course to cover every eventuality, which may or may not relate to your immediate situation.) It is an exciting time, and one that I am embracing both as a consumer and producer. The old classroom model is not the only option for learning. The reason TED Talks have been so successful is because of this trend.

If you are leading a team of people, encourage them to take charge of their own learning by providing them with time and budget to put towards professional development. I have some clients today who give their employees the power to choose how they spend a percentage of their training budget. This is a great idea, because it empowers people, shows that the employer supports their staff in their personal growth and allows for transition into new roles.

8. The power of process

'Making an insanely great product
has a lot to do with the process of making the product
– how you learn things and adopt new ideas
and throw out old ideas.'

Steve Jobs

Processes and systems are an essential part of any successful business or personal venture. They allow you to collapse time, work productively and be agile in your thinking and strategy. They allow you to easily grow and scale your business. Process done well becomes habit, and it's the tried-and-true methods that will make the biggest difference in your ability to create a profitable venture. Once you create a proven process, it doesn't matter who takes it on – that's what makes it so powerful.

Processes and systems are what separate out those that can grow from those who get stuck. When people buy into a franchise, they are buying a set of processes and systems – this takes some of the risk out of the investment, because the processes are tried and tested. Imagine if you could have that power in your own business!

When we first start working towards a big goal or vision, it can take some time to figure out the best way to make things happen. While it's important to set up your systems early (so you can get on track quickly), you might find they shift and develop as you move towards your goal. That's perfectly okay. The important thing is to learn as you go, and make sure you have the flexible mindset required to adjust your processes as needed along the way.

But remember: a system only works if you work the system, the same way a habit only becomes engrained when you are intentional about it.

LEARN FROM THE BEST

Some of the most successful people in business, sport and show-business have understood the power of process. What they all have in common is a constant desire to pursue a better way – always asking questions and being curious about things so they could improve and develop their processes. Let's take a look at how they developed or adopted systems that would work for them.

Steve Jobs

I was lucky enough to work with and for Apple in the mid '90s. While many people associate Apple and its iconic co-founder Steve Jobs with creativity, innovation and design excellence, what many don't know is that Steve had a fanatical desire for process that leads to productivity. In my role as a business development manager for Apple at this time, I learned the power of process – in particular, two specific systems that Apple had adopted from thought leaders Bob Miller and Steve Heiman (Miller Heiman) and Neil Rackham.

Steve also applied his sales and product development systems at his other successful ventures, NeXT Computer and Pixar Animation Studios.

Bill Hewlett and Dave Packard

But where did Steve get inspired about systems? It turns out, as a young man he was friends with Bill Hewlett – co-founder of Hewlett-Packard (HP). Bill and his business partner Dave Packard were known as the 'process kings': they relentlessly pursued excellence, and then mapped each successful process so they could replicate it faster in other products. One of Steve's early jobs was on the production line at HP, assembling IT equipment following a well-defined process. This early learning of process and its importance no doubt led to Steve understanding its power.

Bob Miller and Steve Heiman

When I worked for HP in the late '90s I once again put Miller Heiman systems into practice. Their systems for winning and managing large accounts in the business-to-business sales and marketing space allowed me to excel in my marketing and development role. Sales has a reputation for coming naturally only to those with the 'gift of the gab'. But systems and processes make sales easier for everyone, no matter your level of skill. In developing their systems, Bob Miller and Steve Heiman became curious as to why some of their team members were incredibly successful year after year and could accurately predict their monthly revenue, while others seemed to be on a roller-coaster of sales results and full of 'woulda, coulda, shoulda' excuses. To find out why, Bob and Steve followed their best sales performers and looked at what they did on a day-to-day basis. They then used this data to develop the Miller Heiman sales system, which is still used with success today.

(As a side note: in more recent times, I got to know Bob very well as I represented the Miller Heiman brand for 10 years. I recall having dinner with Bob, who was in his eighties at the time, and we spent some time discussing social media. He was fascinated by the process of gaining Twitter and LinkedIn followers, and how books could be published direct using Amazon. A curious mind with a growth mindset will never grow old!)

Professor Neil Rackham

Professor Neil Rackham is an author, consultant and academic who, like Bob and Steve, also disputed the common myth of born salespeople. Professor Rackham conducted more than 36 000 interviews with salespeople to determine how the most successful managed conversations with customers. From this research he developed his SPIN Selling model (Situation/Problem/Implication/Need-Payoff) and his Insight delivery model.

After all his interviews, Professor Rackham found that it made no difference whether you asked an open or a closed question in a customer conversation. What mattered most was asking the right question of the right person at the right time!

Giacomo Agostini

Let's move to the world of sport, where systems and process are a way of life because you can measure success far more easily, and the need to evolve and test processes happens with every outing.

Giacomo 'Ago' Agostini is an Italian multi-time world champion Grand Prix motorcycle road racer. He has won 18 world championships, most famously riding the iconic Italian brand MV Augusta. Ago is now in his mid seventies, and spends some of his time as an ambassador for the MV Agusta factory. In 2017, I got to meet Ago again after seeing him many years earlier in his heyday in the 1970s. This time, I was interested to see how Ago managed the starting and riding process for the classic MV Agusta for his demo ride at Phillip Island. What I observed was Ago had a specific process and system he used with the MV to ensure all the race-goers got to hear the mighty machine in action: he would start the bike, warm it up and then leave it while he got himself ready. Then he would start the bike up again before shutting it down. Then finally he would start it again before going out on the track. Ago advised race-goers that this process was so important to him that he may have to delay his 'meet and greet' session. He also has a process for his track ride. He gave specific instructions to the commentators to avoid talking during his demo laps, preferring that he and his beloved MV Agusta do all the talking through its magical sound and his precision riding.

Alisa Camplin

'Are you working hard enough when nobody else is watching.'

Alisa Camplin, the Olympic Gold Medallist aerial skier for Australia – and now business leader, philanthropist and mother – had a dream. Her dream since childhood was to win an Olympic Gold Medal for Australia. It wasn't necessarily to win it in skiing. With a burning passion, Alisa just wanted to discover her ultimate potential as an athlete and to become the best in the world. So, she tried a range of sports, from running to gymnastics to sailing, before finally settling on aerial skiing.

Alisa had a dream, now she needed a strategy. Her strategy included selecting a sport that gave her the best possible route to the Gold Medal. Her parameters were as follow:

• It had to be a sport Australia was already world-class at

• It had to be one that was not ridiculously expensive (sailing and dressage with horses were eliminated)

• It had to be one she could do on her own (team sports were out)

• She had to be passionate about it (Alisa explained to me if you can't get passionate about it, then you won't sustain the hard work when things get tough and others start making excuses and falling away)

• There had to be world-class coaching available.

So, after trying several sports, as I mentioned, Alisa finally settled on Olympic aerial skiing. Her next challenge was learning to ski because, at 19 years of age, Alisa did not yet ski!

She then designed a multi-year, goal-planning framework. This comprised milestones and goals based on seven key attributes which, she had discovered, were needed for her to be a world-class aerial skier and viable Gold Medal contender. This process map to gold is one of the most robust, well-structured and intentional roadmaps I have seen. However, without Alisa's absolute commitment to it, and belief in her ability to get it done through some very trying times that would have tested even the most determined of us, this roadmap would have just been a great roadmap.

The lesson is that the process only works if you work the process. Alisa's mindset, adaptability and personal accountability are what made her goal-planning methodology the key to her success. Now a keynote speaker and performance consultant, Alisa says herself, 'A vision without a plan is just a wish'.

AC/DC

As an Australian I was brought up on AC/DC's music. As a good Aussie dad I have subjected my children to their music, too – it's a rite of passage. (Disappointingly, only my middle son, Finn, has come on board.) The lead guitarist, Angus Young, must be faultless as he hits the first chord in front of crowds of hundreds of thousands. Angus does not leave this to chance. He prefers to keep his guitar arsenal on tour to two instruments; he is very specific about what he likes, what works and how things are set up. For over 40 years, the band has maintained the same performing format: Angus on a wireless guitar, roaming around the stage; and Malcolm Young and bass player Cliff Williams on guitars with cables for reliability, positioned near the drummer so they can maintain eye contact to ensure a solid bass and rhythm flow. The reason for this process is not because they are lazy; it is because there are so many variables that are beyond their control, so to deliver an amazing show they need to have a stable, reliable process that works.

Bradley Cooper

Process is essential in showbusiness, too. When Bradley Cooper took on the role of starring in and producing *A Star is Born*, he knew he would need a solid process in order to meet the challenges ahead (not only was it his first directing gig, but Cooper also had to learn to sing to carry off the lead role). Cooper reportedly had a strict schedule he followed day-by-day, including a morning workout, followed by two hours of guitar practice and two hours of piano lessons, then song and screenplay writing in the afternoon. He also practised singing five days a week for several months. If you watch the movie, you will see for yourself just how successful Cooper's process was.

KEEP EVOLVING YOUR PROCESS

A key point to remember with the 4-Step Possibility System© is that it never stops. Once you have mastered a skill, you will find another skill, knowledge area or process that is needed as you grow and evolve. You may need to update your processes or introduce new ones as you go.

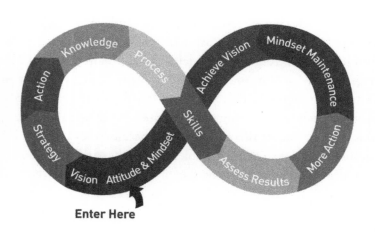

142

9. Developing your skills

'Anyone who stops learning is old, whether at 20 or 80.
Anyone who keeps learning stays young.
The greatest thing in life is to keep your mind young.'

Henry Ford

At this point you might be wondering: what is the difference between knowledge and skills? Put simply, knowledge is the theoretical understanding of something, whereas skills are required for the practical application. For example, when I switched from sailing to cycling I started to gather a lot of information about my new sport by reading magazines, books and websites – this gave me *knowledge* about cycling. But it wasn't until I got out there on the bike and started learning the practical *skills* that I became proficient at it.

FOUR STEPS TO SKILL BUILDING

I am sure you have heard people say, 'you don't know what you don't know'. What they are really saying is that often when you are learning a new skill or mastering a new task you make mistakes, and you are unable to self-correct due to your lack of awareness or experience. We might call this unconscious incompetence – you are making errors, but might not even realise it. Management trainer Martin M Broadwell described the 'four levels of teaching' model in 1969, and it has been used in various forms ever since.

The four stages are:

1. **Unconscious incompetence:** You don't know what you don't know. This is when you try something new, and make 'rookie' errors without even realising.

2. **Conscious incompetence:** At this stage you know what you don't know; you realise through an error, an accident, a fall or mistake. This is when you might feel overwhelmed and say 'this is hard' or 'what have I got myself into'.

3. **Conscious competence:** Now you are getting good, but you really have to focus and prepare to get the task done right. If you lose focus or rush, you will make mistakes.

4. **Unconscious competence:** At this stage, the skill is fully ingrained and you barely have to think about the individual steps involved in performing it. For example, have you ever arrived at a destination and not really remembered driving there? You clearly did, but your mind might not have had to focus on performing the task so was free to think about other things, while your subconscious took care of the skill.

'Four steps to skill building'

M Broadwell, 'Teaching for Learning', *The Gospel Guardian*, February 1969.

Once you know these four steps and you are honest and authentic about your current position, you are well placed to achieve any new skill. But remember, once you have mastered a skill you will soon discover more skills that are needed and start the journey at the bottom of the steps again. You might notice that you become more aware of your unconscious incompetence as you master each skill and grow and evolve. For example, I knew through my sailing that bad habits formed early on become very, very hard to change later in life. When I switched to cycling, I sought coaching so I could prevent early issues becoming major issues later on.

SLOW DOWN TO GO FAST

American motorsports competitor and stunt performer Travis Pastrana was asked on the TV program *Back Page Live* how his riders and performers think so fast during stunts. Travis explained that, in fact, it's the opposite of fast. They actually think through and perform the stunts in slow motion. They need to do this to ensure every detail is right, no small detail is missed and they hit every key acceleration spot, breaking marker or grip change. Travis went on to say that often his riders will spot people in the crowd in detail, even while performing a double back flip!

However, what a crowd does not see is the months and months of setting up the physics and detail behind the jump, the setup of the bike and the hours of practice in foam pits and on practice tracks building up to the main event.

When I started cycling coaching, my coach, David Sturt, said that to go fast in this sport you need to go slow. What he meant was that you need to take the time to build core body strength, technique and muscle resilience. One you have a foundation, you can increase the speed and go to the next level.

This method of slowing down to go fast is also quite common in high-speed sports such as car and motorcycle racing. World champion motorcyclist and TV personality the late Barry Sheene said he often had thoughts about mundane things such as where he had left his car keys while driving down the strait, approaching 250km per hour! Practice and repetition over a 20-year period had trained Barry's brain to feel comfortable operating at these speeds. Formula One race drivers have similar experiences where they are operating at high speeds but able to observe, take in data and make split-second decisions, all because their brain has been trained to do so.

So how does this apply to you? Well, if you want to operate at high speed and achieve a lofty goal or dream you need to build up to it through practice and repetition slowly and then increase up your speed incrementally.

ARE YOU AS GOOD AS YOU THINK?

The Dunning–Kruger effect is a form of cognitive bias in which people mistakenly assess their natural ability as greater than it really is.[11] Essentially what this means is that you might be less competent at a skill than you think you are because you don't know what you don't know.

The flipside is that competent people often underestimate their competency because they think that if a task is easy for them, it must be so for everyone. Consequently, they don't rate their competence as anything special.

This is why I am a huge advocate of coaches and mentors: they will provide you with accurate feedback about your ability and will help you in the areas you need to improve.

FOCUS ON THE RIGHT SKILLS

Adrian Finglas is an Australian sailing champion, Olympic gold medal coach and youth sailing coach. I was fortunate to have Adrian coach me and my sons over a few years in various boats. Alongside the coaching on the water, Adrian took us through some very interesting data related to world-class performance – he says that 85 per cent of high performance is perfection of the basics. For example, in sailing, there are five basic skills that everyone who sails has to perfect:

- Tacking (moving the boat from one direction to the other into the wind)
- Gybing (moving the boat from one direction to the other away from the wind)
- Starting a race
- Mark roundings (turning your boat around the rounding mark while trying to avoid contact with the mark and other boats in the race)
- Tactical decision-making.

Adrian says it takes 10 000 tacks to become world-class. He breaks this down to sailing three times a week for two hours each time, 50 weeks per year. That works out to approximately 11 tacks per hour for each session you do. Now add in 11 gybes, 11 practice starts and 11 mark roundings per hour and it becomes a very packed hour! Also note that in some countries you can't sail 50 weeks of the year (due to weather), so you need to travel. (Are you really willing to pay the price to become world-class?)

If you are in sales or account management, your top five basic skills to perfect might be:

- Connecting with people in person
- Connecting with people by phone
- Collaborating internally in your organisation
- Building proposals
- Presenting proposals.

You can apply Adrian's thinking to this same scenario, or any other situation that reflects your work and goals.

Many world-class organisations are clued in to this concept. I was fortunate to experience the world-class sales training that IBM provides. One of the basic areas they focused on was meeting preparation. They had proven, through data analysis, that people who were well-prepared before a meeting had better meeting outcomes, higher customer satisfaction and generated stronger results for the customer, IBM and themselves. IBM held its staff accountable for meeting preparation, and sales leaders provided coaching in how to properly prepare for meetings – including encouraging staff to book specific meeting preparation time in their calendars to ensure it was done. This is leadership, accountability and discipline in action.

A note for coaches

If we agree there is usually a small handful of skills that make the biggest difference to performance and 85 per cent of world-class performance comes from the perfection of these basics, then the biggest challenge for any coach is how to make the repetitive practice of these fundamentals a continuing learning experience that is interactive, experiential and even entertaining. How often have heard your team say things like:

- Not running again!

- We did drills last week.

- We know how to do role plays.

- I know how to plan for a meeting.

- I was trained in the CRM last week.

- Are we doing hills again?

These phrases often come up when the leader or coach doesn't explain the *why* and the *what* before diving into the *how* of the activity. One of the first things my cycling coaches will always discuss before a drill is why we are doing it and what results we are looking for, either short or long term. Adrian Finglas also does this when he is training groups in sailing. I recall doing a three-hour on-water coaching session with Adrian and a group of like-minded laser dinghy sailors in which we spent the whole time doing all sorts of manoeuvres in a fun and engaging way. After we came in from the very busy but fun session, my wife Leisa was surprised when I told her that all we did for three hours was basically tacking and gybing. The truth is, we barely even realised that's all we were doing, because Adrian made it so enjoyable. Full credit to him – that's why he's a gold medal coach.

I once heard former Australian Football League premiership coach Kevin Sheedy say: 'Practise doesn't make perfect. Perfect practise makes perfect'. All good coaches will tell you this, whether they are in sport or business. Good coaching in world-class habits is the way to scale, and the reason I have always sought out the best possible coaches I could find.

THE POWER OF PLAY

Playing and experimenting is a vital part of skill building. All coaches and instructors will tell you that having informal time to operate outside of the rules, try different things and enjoy the activity you are wanting to build skill in is a vital aspect of improving your competence. It is often in these play sessions that unique, new or innovative ideas and skills are uncovered. With refinement, these can become game changers and often the edge that wins a medal.

All-time great ice hockey player Wayne Gretzky is famous for saying 'you miss 100 per cent of the shots you don't take'.

Wayne was coached by his father in his early years. One of the ways they practised was to use a tennis ball rather than a hockey puck; this was incredibly difficult, but a lot of fun. Gretsky's father was also a strong believer in adaptive game play rather than a strict by-the-playbook approach. These two things combined with Gretzky's passion for the game (which often would see him studying his heroes on screen and replicating the game strategies on paper) assisted with him being one of the greatest players of all time.

National Football League Hall of Fame member the great Jerry Rice was not originally selected as one of the greatest players with promise: he had to fight his way to the top. Rice was eventually known as one of the best receivers in the game. He once said that when he was running for the ball to receive it, it literally slowed down in the air so he could position himself better than his opponent. From a very young age, Jerry would take his football to bed with him and, in the dark, would throw it up in the air and try and catch it without damaging his face. This game had significant payoffs: because he could not see the ball, he had to engage his other senses and learned to listen for the noise the ball made in the air to judge how it was spinning and how fast it was approaching. This skill, combined with the other more formal skills he learned over time, proved to be a formidable combination.

Nine-time world motorcycle champion Valentino Rossi is well known for his 'Ranch': a private training track at his home in Italy. The Ranch features a fast and flowing gravel track, where he invites racing friends and team members to come and play. The idea of the gravel is that the bike moves around much more, so you have to learn to slide it and have it move around underneath you at speed in order to master the track.

Australian sailing champion Tom Burton won the gold medal at the Rio Olympics using a technique he had perfected as a young boy growing up sailing on Lake Macquarie. Through childhood play, Tom became a master of sailing his boat backwards, and used this skill with great effect to position himself perfectly on the start line – leaving his opponent in a penalty situation while Tom sailed off cleanly to pursue victory.

One of the world's most celebrated and popular soccer players is Pelé. On the streets of São Paulo, Brazil, as a young boy, Pelé developed his famous ball-handling skills. Growing up in a disadvantaged neighbourhood, he did not have football fields to play on – just the street, laneways, stairwells and other obstructions that provided a perfect playground to hone his skills.

So, how do you apply the principle of play at work? One way is to be less afraid of failure. Adopting an attitude of play means giving things a go, trying something new and experimenting with different ideas. Motorcycle racers will tell you that if you aren't falling off every so often you are not trying hard enough; if you are not trying and failing at work, you are not growing and learning.

US entrepreneur Paul Martinelli says that the fastest way he learned to grow a new business was to have regular 'failure meetings'. At a failure meeting, everyone who attends must bring along at least one example of a new idea or strategy they tried and failed at, and share the learning. For failure meetings to work you must already have developed an environment of psychological safety. People must feel comfortable trying, failing, learning and trying again. If you can do this, you will grow your results exponentially and everyone will grow and learn as a team. You also need to be comfortable with vulnerability. Celebrate the sharing and the learning, and focus on the growth mindset that your team is demonstrating by trying new things. You might also like to keep a learning log: an online or offline record of all the things tried and learned.

HOW TO INFLUENCE PEOPLE

A lot of the skills you need will be specific to your area of development, but there are some important skills that all successful people must work to perfect. One of these is influencing skills.

The first thing to know about influencing is: you can't influence people unless you have credibility. You must take your credibility seriously if you want to be an influencer, and you need to be able to influence if you want to achieve your vision.

Your reputation – or personal brand, if you like – is one of the most valuable assts you will ever have. A credible reputation is earned. You are not born with it, but it lingers on after you have gone. Over the years I have come to develop a strategy for building credibility, because I see it as a lifelong pursuit. The model I use is based on John C Maxwell's 'three Cs' model: character, competence and credibility.[12] I have added a fourth element: care factor. Here's what they mean:

- **Character:** Can people trust you? Are you reliable and authentic? Do you do what you say you will? Are you accountable and willing to go the extra mile for someone? What is your track record with helping others? Do people recommend you?

- **Competence:** Do you have capability, knowledge and expertise in what you do?

- **Connections:** Are you part of at least one community? Do you make a conscious effort to connect with people, both in person and online? Do you make an effort to maintain the connections you have?

- **Care factor:** Do you really care about people, or do you just look for what they can do for you? Are you genuine? Do you care about your team? Do you care about your area of expertise?

How would you rate yourself? More importantly, how do you think others would rate you? A 360 degree feedback assessment (where you seek feedback from your direct reports, co-workers and manager) can you give you an idea, however there are other ways to get a feel for your credibility. Try answering these questions:

- When people have issues in your area of expertise, do they come to you for assistance?
- When people need to talk to someone they can trust, do they come to you first?
- Do people invite you to events? Do they come to yours?
- Do people seek you out on social media, and do they accept your requests?

Influence in action

The first factor in influencing people is that you must know what you want. We are all familiar with SMART (specific, measurable, achievable, realistic and time-based) goal setting – use it to help you identify exactly what it is you are hoping to gain.

I use the SWAWSE acronym to help guide my influencing:

S   SMART goal setting

W   Who do you need to influence?

A   What actions/behaviours do you want them to take/ develop?

W   Will they be willing to do what you're asking?

S   Do they have the skills to do what you're asking?

E   Is their environment encouraging?

My son, Finn, recently used this model when he was making a short film as part of an assignment. Here's how he went:

S   He needed to have his short movie completed by 30 October.

W   He needed to influence friends to take the acting roles, teachers to allow him to film after hours and to appear in the movie and his brother to lend him camera equipment.

A   He needed the students and teachers to find time in their busy schedules to study the script and rehearse. He needed everyone to be passionate about his vision.

W   He needed to encourage their willingness by ensuring they were part of the vision, agreed on the script and add their input to bring the characters alive.

S   He needed to ensure participants could read a script, act their part and take direction.

E   He needed to recruit actors and teachers who already had an interest in filmmaking and dramatic arts, and who thrived in a creative setting.

HONING YOUR COMMUNICATION SKILLS

'The single biggest problem in communication is the illusion that it has taken place.'

George Bernard Shaw

We are all affected in different ways by communication. Communication takes several forms: it could be visual, auditory or kinaesthetic (tactile). Think about a time you have gone to a concert with friends, and afterwards asked, 'what did you think?'. You probably got a variety of answers:

- What a great concert! Did you see the lead singer ...

- What a great sound! I loved the amazing guitar solo ...

- What a great concert! The atmosphere and the crowd was incredible ...

The take-home message, as any performer knows, is that you must deliver communication in a variety of ways so that it connects visually, auditorily and emotes a feeling. This is why storytelling is so powerful, and will always be an important skill to develop.

When I am planning to communicate an important message, there are three things I'm thinking of:

- **Feel:** How do I want the recipient of my communication to feel? We may not remember everything we hear, but we humans are very good at remembering how we felt in any given situation. I have seen comedian Arj Barker live several times, and while I can't remember all of his jokes now, I can remember feeling fantastic after each of his sets. So much of our communication, especially if we are speaking on behalf of a large company or corporation, is sanitised to the point that it loses all authenticity and feeling. If your communications are described as 'boring', you can bet that people will not remember your message.

- **Know:** At the end of my communication (whether it be delivered via a meeting, phone call or email), what do I want the other party to know and understand? What are three specific pieces of information or insight you want to convey? (Any more than three to five key insights is information overload, so keep it brief.)

- **Do:** At the end of the interaction, what do you want the other party to do? You should never assume people know what you want them to do after you have spoken; you need to be specific. This does not mean demanding things of people, but you do need to provide them with options or a path to follow.

COMMUNICATING ACROSS CHANNELS

Depending on your vision, you will need to be proficient in communicating using a variety of different methods and channels (or at least have a team you can call on to help). The following channels are the most common and important:

Speaking

You need to be able to speak confidently and effectively in front of an audience – whether this is your team, your colleagues or a theatre full of people. I know a lot of you, given the choice, would rather be the one in the casket than the one delivering the eulogy at a funeral – but it doesn't have to be like this. Nobody is born a natural speaker, and even the best of the best speakers have tough days where not everything works out. However, there is an art and a science to speaking, just as there is an art and a science to possibility. If you're not a confident speaker, seek out a coach or a course to develop your skills. I wish for you to be good speakers because I know you have great stories that the world needs to hear – or if not the world, at least your family and friends. (As a side note, older speakers often tell me that later life is a wonderful time for learning to speak, as the older you get the more stories there are to tell – and fewer people are around who remember the truth! You are never too old to learn anything.)

Speaking can also mean one-on-one communication, either face-to-face, over the phone or via video. This is a different skill to speaking to an audience, because it usually demands good listening skills, too. My biggest tip here is to be curious, and practice active listening. Having a sense of curiosity about people, innovation and ideas is an easy way to connect with people. If you do this authentically, you will ask intelligent questions and listen effectively because you are interested in the answer.

Learning to be comfortable with silence is another skill we all need to work hard on. With so much noise in and around us, it's like we are programmed to respond immediately to any question – even if we didn't hear it properly. How many times have you found yourself waiting for the other person to finish so you could jump in with what you want to say, irrespective of what they just said? A sales training colleague of mine told me a story of when he was fresh out of university and new to communicating with clients. One Monday he met with a new customer and asked her how her weekend was. She quietly replied that her father had passed away over the weekend. He responded on autopilot, saying 'Fantastic, that's great, I had a busy weekend too' – at the same time as his brain was saying, 'What did she just say?'. Unfortunately, he was too late: the damage was done and he lost the account. Since then, he has made a huge effort to learn the technique of active listening.

Writing

All communication skills are a matter of practice. The subtlety is understanding that we are in an age where we must be able to pivot quickly to learn, unlearn and relearn. This is exactly what happened to me with this book. I can write. But writing for speaking or for a proposal or for website copy is not the same as writing a book. It had been 12 years since I had written my last book, so I had to relearn this craft. My editor and especially my publisher encouraged me to speed this process up, after seeing the first draft of this book. (You are lucky you are reading this version. Yikes, I was even struggling reading my first version!)

Even if you are not writing a book, writing is an effective skill to have – particularly in this age, where so much communication happens via email. If your skills in this area are not up to scratch, it's time to invest in a course or do some research online to learn how to communicate effectively using the written word. Or, if there is someone in your team who is an excellent email communicator, why not ask them for some tips, or see if they would be willing to provide some constructive feedback on your written communication?

Social media

It's not an option to avoid this one, no matter what your age. If you want to influence people, you need to get familiar with using the social media platforms that best suit your business. This doesn't mean you need to be active on every single platform, if that doesn't suit you – it's best to choose the ones where your target audience hang out, and work on perfecting those. (Plus LinkedIn, which I think is mandatory for every professional.)

If social media really isn't your thing, is it possible to outsource this task? If not, there is plenty of free information on the web that will help you to communicate effectively via whichever platforms you choose.

COACHING

'When you feel like you are trapped
in a box of potential and can't seem to break out,
and you know the instructions to getting out
are on the outside of the box,
this is when you most need a coach.'

Paul Martinelli

Coaches are critical to fast-tracking success. It amazes me how many people expect to make dramatic shifts or pursue a lofty goal without the help of a coach or mentor.

Before you hire a coach, it's important to ask yourself the following question: 'Am I coachable?'. Being coachable means you are open to learning, receiving feedback, making changes and listening. If you don't have a track record of doing this, then working with a coach will be difficult. It is very important that you and your coach can work together for the success of both parties.

A good coach will help you in the following ways:

- They collapse time by suggesting shortcuts from their experience
- They prevent errors from occurring due to your lack of experience (not knowing what you don't know)
- They prevent bad strategies or techniques from becoming habits
- They keep you accountable
- They add value to your pursuits.

When selecting a coach, make sure you choose someone who is going to add value because they know more than you. That is, they should have achieved something you have not, or be more qualified than you are. You are paying for their guidance and accountability, but also for their experience and capability, so there is no point choosing someone who is on the same level as you.

I have found the best coaches to be the ones you have to apply to; that is, they don't take on just anyone, and they know who their ideal coachee is. When I hired public relations coach Kate Engler, I had to go through three application rounds before she took me on. It was quite a journey to even get to speak with her.

Was it worth it? Absolutely, because Kate applies the same rigour to her coaching practice as she does to her application process.

When I approached my cycling coach David 'Steggles' Sturt, he didn't just sign me up – we had a consultation, then a training ride and then a discussion around my bike setup, and only when I agreed to set up my bike in the way Steggles suggested did he take me on. This might seem like 'tough love', but I think it's a sign of a great coach when they take the time to be sure you're the right candidate before they agree to have you on their team.

Good coaches who focus on consistent, sustainable high-level performance always give more than you pay for. The best ones provide so many other skills that are transferable to a range of other areas of your life. One of the best examples of this in action is my sons' former motocross coach, Glenn 'Macca' Macdonald. Macca taught his young riders more than just riding and racing skills: he had them learn about nutrition, the importance of sleep, mechanics and media skills. Many of the skills my son Ben was taught by Macca he was able to apply to sailing when he changed to that sport, and to other areas of his life as well.

If you are coachable, you will probably find that coaches also find you. Often we miss out on connecting with potential coaches because we are so focused on something else. In one cycling criterium I was put in A grade for a masters race. I was in no way ready for A grade, but thought I would give it a go. I survived for 30 minutes and was then dropped; I just could not keep up. However, in the first 20 minutes I was hanging in there, when one of the serious contenders, Adam Hawkins, dropped back and gave me some quick tips. He then took off again and won the race. If that was not impressive enough, he found me on Facebook and wrote me a serious of tips of how I could improve and avoid some basic rookie errors I had made. Not only was this unexpected and very generous of Adam, it motivated me to have a go again which I did.

When you are working with a coach, remember you are working with them in a specific area in which they have resources and knowledge you can benefit from. It is important to realise that no-one is perfect in every area of their life. For example, just because I work with a fantastic speaking coach does not mean they have their entire life in order and nor does it matter. If you focus on the whole person you will lose momentum in their coaching and advice, and find excuses not to use their advice when things become hard. Don't make judgement calls outside of the expertise you have hired your coach for.

Coaches versus mentors

So what's the difference between a coach and a mentor, and which one do you need? Simply put, coaches focus on coaching you in a particular skill or set of skills, whereas mentors focus on improving you as a person, which may from time to time include skill development. Coaching typically follows a structured format, whereas mentoring is often more informal. My son Ben is lucky enough to be mentored by Alistair Murray AM. Alistair has seen Ben blossom in his media business and is keen to help him grow. Alistair has vast commercial business experience and offered his time and guidance to connect with Ben on a regular basis to check in with his progress and answer questions he may have as a young business owner.

Mentors don't have to physically connect with you. They may provide guidance and advice on your personal journey through online workshops, books and podcasts these days. However, there must be a common connection; they must have achieved something you wish to in business, life, sport or relationships. Mentor-mentee relationships should always be built on credibility and trust.

From bikes to boats: the power of coaching

When my oldest son, Ben, was four, I bought him his first dirt bike: a Yamaha PW50. Ben loved it, and by age five he was racing it whenever we had a spare weekend. It was clear he enjoyed it and had some talent – certainly way more than me at that age – so we went all-in and I stopped sailing so we could focus on racing junior motocross. Probably the biggest change was for Leisa, who had to get involved in a sport that was completely foreign to her. She was a corner marshal, which involved having 30 or so kids coming at her riding motorcycles that were more powerful than most small cars.

As Ben got older his bikes got faster, the jumps became bigger and we became more nervous each time he raced. When he reached age 12, we made the decision to move back to sailing. This was a big shift for Ben, but it really helped that we supported him with the right coaches who shared the same views on leadership, discipline and accountability that Ben had experienced in motocross. We trained with Sorrento Sailing, Couta Boat Club and Sandringham Yacht Club, and worked with inspirational coaches such as Scott Llewellyn, two times Olympian and multiple world champion Sarah Blanck, Mark Tonner-Joyce, Oli Tweddell and Johnny Rogers. The result was that Ben went from competing at state level in motocross at age 12 to winning the Victorian Youth Championships in the competitive Laser class at age 16 and competing in two world championships. That's the power of good coaching.

Coaching your team

Coaching your team (whether that be within the organisation you work for, your family, your own company or even your kids' sports club) requires a whole separate skill set you will need to develop. When you have a team, you need to make sure its members are growing and improving. I like to use the GROW model, except I add an extra 'S' to the start and finish:

S What is the subject of the coaching session?

G What is the goal we are looking to achieve?

R What is the current reality?

O What are the options and opportunities?

W What will be the next steps and actions?

S Self-reflection for the coach.

I believe the final 'S' is one of the most important. As a coach, it's important that you self-reflect on the session – how it went and what you could do better next time. Then imagine that moment again implementing what you have decided, so the subconscious mind remembers the best practice and not the error.

Final thoughts

'Stop comparing yourself to other people.
You're only on this planet to be you,
not someone else's imitation of you ...
Your life journey is about learning to become
more of who you are and fulfilling the highest,
truest expression of yourself.'

Oprah Winfrey

Life is simple, but we complicate it. Simplicity is the key above all else. That doesn't mean it's easy – nothing worth having ever is. But that doesn't mean it is all hard work, either. When you have passion, it doesn't feel like work – you are in flow, and flow is a beautiful thing.

If you are still procrastinating, that's okay, too. Keep thinking. Keep reflecting. Give yourself time to go through this process, and don't feel guilty or worry about what others think. But remember: the best way to break free from procrastination is to take action. Do something, learn something, help someone, visit someone, love someone. Most of all, love yourself, as Lance Picioane's Love Me Love You suggests. The simple truth is that you can't give what you don't have. If you don't love who you are, then you can't give love to anybody else.

If you want to make a change in your life but you're feeling overwhelmed, look at the 4 Steps and select the one you need to focus on first; the one that will make the biggest difference.

Then, take action with personal leadership, discipline and determination. If you do this consistently you will make significant progress, and you will achieve your vision sooner than you thought was possible. Then you will discover your next calling, and start this exciting process again – but this time, you will be even better at it. How cool is that!

In closing, I wish it all for you. I really do. The world needs your ideas, your inspiration, your business, your designs, your movies, your technology. Don't give up. Persist. I wish that you achieve all you want to achieve in this wonderful life that you and I were uniquely designed for.

Stay kind, respect each other and above all, keep smiling!

Recommended reading

ONLINE

Rob Hartnett
robhartnett.com
youtube.com/robhartnettlive
Instagram @robhartnett
Twitter @robhartett
facebook.com/thepossibilityguy
Art of the Possible podcast on iTunes and Spotify

Knights of Suburbia
knightsofsuburbia.com

Love Me Love You/Lance Picioane
lovemeloveyou.org.au

Aaron Wood
mobilepersonaltrainerlanecove.com.au

Nathanael Zurbrügg
nathanaelzurbruegg.com

Dr Hannah MacDougall
hannahmacdougall.com.au

Lee Turner
Instagram @_leeturner

Alisa Camplin
alisacamplin.com

David Sturt
www.thehurtbox.com

BOOKS

Russell Brand *Mentors*

Professor Carol Dweck *Mindset: Changing the Way You Think to Fulfil Your Potential*

Fiori Giovanni *Defy Your Destiny*

Dr David Hawkins *Letting Go: The Pathway to Surrender*

Rachel Hollis *Girl, Stop Apologizing*

James Kouzes and Barry Posner *The Leadership Challenge*

Angela Lee-Duckworth *Grit: The Power of Passion and Perseverance*

John C Maxwell *Developing the Leader Within You 2.0* and *Put Your Dream to the Test*

Bob Miller and Stephen Heiman *Strategic Selling: The Unique Sales System Proven Successful by America's Best Companies*

Hans Rosling *Factfulness: How to Really Understand the Modern World*

Peter Sagan *My World*

Eric Schmidt, Jonathan Rosenberg and Alan Eagle *Trillion Dollar Coach: The Leadership Handbook of Silicon Valley's Bill Campbell*

Roger Wells, *Happy to Burn: Meditation to Energize Your Spirit*

Rosamund Stone Zander and Benjamin Zander, *The Art of Possibility: Transforming Professional and Personal Life*

Endnotes

1   Lifeline, 'Statistics on Suicide in Australia',
    www.lifeline.org.au.

2   Bronnie Ware, 'Regrets of the dying', bronnieware.com.

3   P Lally et al. 'How are habits formed: Modelling habit
    formation in the real world', *European Journal of Social
    Psychology*, vol. 40, no. 6, 2009.

4   G Vaynerchuk, instagram.com/garyvee.

5   M Rennex, '6 things we learned from our tour with Julie
    Bishop', *Business Chicks*, businesschicks.com.

6   D Hawkins, *Letting Go: The Pathway of Surrender*, 2013.

7   Based in part on the work of M Homer, *Uncommon Sense:
    The Popular Misconceptions of Business, Investing and Finance
    and How to Profit by Going Against the Tide*, John Murray
    Learning, 2017.

8   J Kouzes and B Posner, *The Leadership Challenge: How
    to Make Extraordinary Things Happen in Organizations*,
    Wiley, 2012.

9   Strava, '2018 Year In Sport', strava.com.

10 A Kramer and K Erickson, *Hippocampus*, 2009.

11 J Kruger and D Dunning, 'Unskilled and unaware of it:
    How difficulties in recognizing one's own incompetence lead
    to inflated self-assessments', *Journal of Personality and Social
    Psychology*, Vol 77(6), 1999.

12 Maxwell, *The 21 Irrefutable Laws of Leadership: Follow Them
    and People Will Follow You*, HarperCollins, 2007.

Index

A percentage of the sales of this book will be donated to the Knights of Suburbia Cycling and Love Me, Love You Foundation to raise awareness of mental health and help prevent youth suicide.

Knights of Suburbia

Knights of Suburbia is a community of women and men with a passion for cycling – whether it be crit racing, commuting or coffee-shop rolling. The Knights of Suburbia cycle for physical and mental health, for the sense of community, for adventure and most importantly, for fun. But what unites them is their mission and sense of purpose: to change the culture around mental health by raising awareness, stopping the stigma, starting conversations and empowering people to develop wellbeing and resilience in overcoming life's challenges.

> *We roll deep.*
> *We roll for body. We roll for mind.*
> *We roll for ourselves. We roll for others.*
> *We roll together. We roll apart.*
> *But when we roll, we know*
> *We're never alone.*

Love Me Love You

Love Me Love You is a non-profit organisation that strives to empower and build resilience in young adults so that they can overcome the stigma surrounding mental illness and other life hardships. Almost one in four young Australians are unhappy with their lives. Due to the lack of awareness and the stigma surrounding mental health and substance abuse, many young adults choose to face their battles alone.

A former first-round draft pick and AFL footballer, Lance Picioane established Love Me Love You in 2013 to help young adults take control of their mental wellbeing and to live happier, more fulfilling lives. As a teenager and throughout his AFL career, Lance suffered from depression and anxiety. Like many young adults, Lance chose not to ask for help, but instead turned to partying and substance abuse.

By being truthful with himself, his family and his friends, Lance turned a corner and sought help. Although he still has his down days, Lance now lives a life full of love and happiness. Love Me Love You programs are based on Lance's experiences and are aimed at educating young adults about the importance of mental health and empowering youths to Get Back to School, Back to Sport, Back to Life!

An incredibly relatable and down-to-earth character, Lance and Love Me Love You have touched people from all walks of life through ongoing community initiatives such as the annual 'March with Me' walk, as well as hosting several workshops and ongoing events across Victoria.

Empowering young adults to reach their potential in life.
By fostering a positive change through awareness, education and acceptance we can begin to remove the stigma associated with mental health, drugs, alcohol, eating disorders and life hardships.